Occupation: Self-Employed

Occupation: Self-Employed

Rosemary Pettit

Wildwood House London

First published 1977

Wildwood House Ltd
29 King Street
London WC2E 8JD

ISBN hardback 0 7045 0238 0
paperback 0 7045 0239 9

IBM set by Supreme Litho Typesetting, Romford, Essex.
Printed and bound in Great Britain by Biddles Limited, Guildford, Surrey.

Acknowledgments

To all the many people who have given so generously of their time and experience. Without their help and encouragement this book would have been impossible to write. Thanks also to my editors, Dieter Pevsner and Oliver Caldecott, for their initial imagination and continued support.

Contents

Introduction

Not everybody in this book is making a fortune, very few are. The most convincing reason for being self-employed, however, has very little to do with money and much more to do with how one chooses to spend one's life. Being self-employed is being responsible for all aspects of one's working life: to be producer, salesman, accountant and tea-maker all in one. It is having control over both the quality of the product at one end and the marketing of it at the other. From society's point of view the self-employed, whether freelance journalist or small businessman, is a viable and essential alternative to work within the giant industries of state, union and corporate enterprise. The self-employed do not fill up dole queues, nor do they need underpinning by subsidies; they tend to create work rather than otherwise.

To accept self-employment is to accept the development and exercise of a wide range of skills and abilities, abilities which often atrophy within the departmental confines of a large organization. It is also to accept that if you, personally, do not go vigorously to work, then nothing gets done and no money comes in. If the work isn't good enough then bills do not get paid. If judgment and planning are faulty you go out of business. For most self-employed people there is a small margin of error; go beyond that and you could say goodbye to independence. Bristow, that lovable, idle buying clerk, would not survive two minutes if he had to fend for himself.

The self-employed sector of the economy is also bureaucratically untidy – an open-ended, adaptable situation which we might welcome but which governments find annoying. More through heavy-handedness than malice they have overloaded the self-employed desk with quantities of brown envelopes which, though time-wasting, do at least foster ingenuity and endurance. That's not all. Working for yourself is not work for everybody nor perhaps should it be. Resourcefulness, flexibility, capacity for hard work – all those sort of excellent qualities are needed (as, ideally, they are in any form of work), plus a willingness to take decisions on many levels. Some types of work are, naturally, more demanding and stretching than others.

Ask anybody why they work for themselves and, more often than not, they look into the middle distance and mumble something like, 'Why not?' It is probably more useful to ask, 'How does it work out?' This is what this book has attempted to discover, individual by individual. It is a book intended for anybody who may be in a position to work for themselves and it sets out to show how one person earns his or her livelihood without, in most cases, much capital, previous expertise or prima donna talents. (Some livelihoods, it has to be said, are potential rather than actual.) It is a story which can be multiplied with infinite variety throughout the country; here is one small slice of the cake. It is a taste rather than a recipe book (look in the bibliography for that), a flavour rather than a minute analysis of the ingredients. It aims attention at the successful (or at any rate the surviving) rather than those who have fallen flat on the ground. It is intended to be encouraging.

I interviewed about sixty self-employed people in the first six months of 1976. They represent a wide, though not exhaustive, range of occupations. Each one is an individual and approaches his or her work from an individual standpoint; this approach is not easily extrapolated into another, perhaps completely different, situation. Nevertheless, each particular story can be indicative of the occupation as a whole provided that individual variables of ability, inclination and personal and financial resources are taken into account.

At the end of each section is a postscript dating from October 1976. This is followed by a short summary which sets out the main capital and financial requirements of the business very briefly and as a guideline only. The three groups of income need explaining: A is up to £1,800; B is from £1,800 to £3,000; and C is from £3,000. Working capital is not included in the summary; this should always be added to the figures given. The summary usually applies only to that particular business and no other. Addresses at the back of the book are included for follow-up research.

It is not really for me to say how this book should be used, but I would read the whole of it at some time or other rather than pick and choose. Individuals, reflecting on their own work, often make observations whose implications go well beyond the range of their immediate environment and some occupations previously rejected or ignored may reveal hidden highlights. Some need particular talents but most are accessible to a fair number of people. This book is by no means the last word on anything but, if used as a springboard, could encourage you, the prospective self-employer, to take that step.

Groups of Income Referred to in Text		
A	–	up to £1,800
B	–	from £1,800 to £3,000
C	–	from £3,000

Chapter One
Plants & Animals

HORTICULTURE

A large garden and a greenhouse = space: space to feed a family on home-grown vegetables or space to grow plants for sale – or both. Clare S, an enthusiastic gardener, started experimenting with her sixteen by eight foot greenhouse the minute it was put up two years ago. 'I grew courgettes in jiffy pots,' she says, 'and the surplus ones I took to an iron-monger's shop. I was to come back the next day and either collect the plants or take away the money. They went in ten minutes.' This was encouraging and she pottered away throughout the summer until, in October, a neighbour came in with her and they grew and sold lupins, polyanthus and two thousand wallflowers in boxes. Neither of the partners made much money; in fact they only cleared £10 profit each during the first year, because 'we didn't charge for our time at all,' says Clare S. 'We both loved doing it and we virtually gave them away to our friends because we didn't like selling them. Everybody said we must charge more; we only charged half the usual price just to get a quick turnover.'

In the spring of 1975 a previous customer, delighted with the wallflowers, asked them to supply her garden for her daughter's wedding. 'It was tremendous for us,' says Clare S. 'We worked about twelve hours a day growing everything she wanted from petunias to lobelia to alyssum to sweet peas. It was through her that people started ringing up and saying "Do you have this, do you have that?".' Once the greenhouse was rid of bedding plants they tried house plants ('hopefully to flower from October onwards'), perennials, herbs and vegetables, which are 'the biggest thing at the moment because they're so expensive in the shops'.

Then a new, green-fingered neighbour joined them. With three partners the business flourished. 'We've expanded about twenty times,' says Clare S. 'The demand is fantastic and we're now supplying about three garden centres. Again, how do you get into these places? I went down with some samples and the chap said, "Fine, what else have you got?" I told him. He ordered things in hundreds. He wanted three hundred parsley plants; he wanted all the herbs.' Friends are still the main customers but Clare S, who does most of the selling, prefers to sell to garden centres and the occasional shop. 'I was terrified of selling the first year,' she says. 'But I now enjoy it because our stuff is just as good as anything they get from the huge places.' The local garage is another customer and has taken three hundred tomato plants this season.

In its third year the business has become more commercial; prices reflect this as well as working methods. Quite early on Clare S found a wholesaler who supplies virtually all their pots, boxes and earth. It is essential to buy from a wholesaler, she says, to cut costs right down. Seeds are another expense. This year plants are germinated from their own seed. Instead of growing all and everything Clare S is beginning to specialize, which she would recommend. 'Don't be as ambitious as we were and try to do so many things at once; we got in such a muddle. Label everything the minute you've done it,' she says, 'otherwise you forget.' A greenhouse is essential; hers cost £300.

The business is not going to make any of them rich. Each partner should clear £200 income by the end of the season. Clare S has estimated that she earns less than agricultural

wages working part-time. So how far can they expand? 'Mainly it's a space problem,' she says. 'Even with our three gardens we've run out of space. My first partner is going to minimize the work because she is older and finds it quite a strain. It's not an old person's pastime unless you're retired and simply have nothing else to do. It works very well with children at school and I work while they play in the garden. I always thought that when my youngest was at school I would get a job of some sort, but I never dreamt it would be this. The real satisfaction is doing something which you like, which started as a hobby, and actually making money out of it.'

Four months later
'We're now supplying four garden centres,' says Clare S, 'and a local shop which has bought all the herbs. Perennials and vegetables are the main thing; there's no money in annuals at all. We don't initiate varieties of plants, we just supply the demand.'

Part-time
Capital: greenhouse cost £300
 paraffin to heat greenhouse in winter costs £25
 ¼ acre garden (between all three partners)
 car essential
Income: A
Qualifications: none

FARMING

i. General

Anthony R lives in the midst of an idyll. The sun pours down on the tender green wheat, lambs gambol in tune with tradition, cows chew, the mill grinds his flour, the loom weaves his wool and he and his family live off their own butter, cheese, honey and half an acre of dew-sprinkled vegetables. He is a farmer. The other side of the picture is in the middle of a wet and freezing night, bogged down in a clay pudding of soggy potatoes. There are more romantic conceptions about farming or living off the land than about any other occupation. Anthony R receives a regular stream of starry hopefuls, about to buy a cottage and a few acres, seeking his advice. From a lifetime of experience this is what he has to say.

The first thing he stresses is previous experience, 'spending five years full-time working on somebody else's farm. You will see how it is done, year in, year out, learning by somebody else's mistakes. What is interesting about agriculture is that after a year you think you know it all, up to two years you realize you know very little and after five years you know quite a bit and can start on your own with a fair amount of confidence.' Going to college, he says, is no substitute for experience.

Without that experience farming can be a very expensive mistake. In any case it is expensive. Although the quality and price of land vary enormously from one part of the country to another, Anthony R says, 'it is very difficult to make a living in general agriculture under fifty acres. People think they'll buy a smallholding; they say, "I'll sell my house in London and it will buy a small farm in Wales," but it won't capitalize it. The smallest tractor, new, is nearly £2,000 and an absolute necessity.' So how much money would one need? 'Something in the rate of £40,000,' he says, 'absolute minimum to start with, unless one of them is going to keep on a well-paid job.'

There is a considerable difference between farming for a living, though, and self-sufficiency farming. Anthony R explains it this way: 'To keep yourself and your family in food and clothes and shelter you would only need ten to fifteen acres and you could start off with not much more than the capital for the place. From the self-sufficiency angle it is probably better just to go ahead and look over the hedge and see what the man is doing next door and go and help him. It's all hard labour after that, a great joy if you have the mental and physical capacity for it.'

Clearly a farmer has to be strong and healthy, but his attitude of mind is equally important. 'It's the capacity to keep on with something that seems very unproductive at the time,' says Anthony R. 'So many jobs are like the one I had this afternoon, which is paring the sheep's feet. It isn't making the sheep grow faster, it isn't helping them to have more lambs, but it is absolutely essential if the sheep are going to live.'

More than anything, it seems, farming is team work, especially family team work. 'Anyone who tries to do any form of agriculture without a competent wife – well, it's impossible,' he declares. 'It isn't so much the work that they do on the farm as the fact that when you come in, tired and hungry and fed-up, there's some food and some shelter and some love waiting for you.' Aside from that there are family expectations to reckon with. 'What makes it difficult for many people,' he says, 'is that they come into farming from a job where they earned £60 or £100 a week and the thought that they're going to live on £10 or £14 for the next so many years doesn't seem possible. They are so busy that they don't have time to spend any money anyway and they just have to live off their farms. A farmer who is not feeding well is a contradiction.'

The cautionary tale below (page 6) shows how easy it is to become unstuck.

Full-time

Capital: £40,000 of which premises might cost £25,000; machinery £7,500;
stock £7,500
full-time worker (age 20 and over) £36.50 (January 1976) a week

Income: variable

'In a period of five years, for three years the farm keeps the farmer, for two years the farmer keeps the farm.'
Qualifications: five years' practical experience

Subsistence
Capital: £20,000 for house and land
family assistance
Income: in kind
Qualifications: none

ii. Geese

Nick W has bred geese for the last three years. This year might be his last. Every day he collects buckets of eggs and puts them in the incubator, but every day he has to feed most of them to the pigs. The eggs are infertile and nobody knows why. The vet doesn't know why; nor do the National Farmers' Union, the Ministry of Agriculture, the British Waterfowl Association and other goose farmers. Everybody is very interested in the problem: it could be a virus, it could be the food, it could be anything. Meanwhile, instead of ten thousand goslings, which would have given him and his wife a year's income, only three hundred had been born by halfway through the season.

Breeding geese is a notoriously risky business – a high-risk, high-return venture. Growing only one kind of 'crop' is also risky, leaving nothing to cushion you if it should fail. Nick W knew all this when he started but, he says, 'What else can you do in the country with seven acres and £3,000 borrowed capital? You can either build helicopters at Yeovil or sell bras at Somerton or get your patch of land and try and squeeze a living out of it.' So geese it was. He bought a hundred birds from Denmark and in their first year feed prices doubled, but they sorted out the teething problems and all seemed fair for the next year. Then disaster struck: very few fertile eggs. They changed banks, trebled the stock, brought in new ganders and the same thing happened again this year. So, owing £10,000 to the bank, Nick W may have to sell the house and seven acres unless 'men with microscopes' can very quickly find a solution.

In retrospect, what could he have done? 'The same thing,' he says, 'but started sooner. It would have cost a lot less especially if you've hocked your house and land for the privilege of making those mistakes.' Wouldn't it be better to start small? 'No, because the geese were designed to produce a full year's income and it would have done me no good at all to produce a dozen goslings now and again. We had enquiries this year for thirty thousand goslings. There's a tremendous market if you can produce them.' So where does the difficulty lie? 'This is a completely new problem that has never been met in any poultry in this country before,' he says. 'There's a chance that it's not food or a virus but bad management, farming without the background. There are few precedents for this type of farming whereas the overall principles for running a small, mixed farm are firmly laid down. An established farmer, though, would be well aware of the dangers which could make or break him.'

Nick W bought his house and land in the middle of Somerset for £5,200 five or six years ago. At that time he was working in electrical engineering, but gradually he gave that up and started keeping goats. Goats led to cheese and cheese led to sales in London: Cranks, Ceres, Harrods, Wholefood. The seasonal aspect was a problem: with nothing to sell in the winter, apple picking and working in a local stables helped to augment their income. After a while petrol prices went up, feed prices went up and there was a retail price freeze. Goats faded away and in came geese. There is always another possibility, as Nick W admits: 'The other alternative is to sit on your croft growing lettuces for yourself, but it's virtually impossible, you can't cut yourself off from the world. Anyway, who wants to go back three hundred years? I quite like modern comforts such as the radio and paraffin heater!'

Six months later
The mystery of the ailing geese remains unsolved, though it is thought it could be a disbalance between the calcium-phosphate ratio in the food. Nick W is selling his house and has enough change in his pocket to buy a cottage in the next village. He has enrolled at the local technical college to re-take his A levels and has been accepted for a veterinary course next year.

Full-time
Capital: land £5,200
£3,000 borrowed from bank at beginning, enough for one hundred geese
geese cost £3 each (1974) and £12 a year to feed
incubator £1,000
car essential
Income: C (intended)
Qualifications: none

BEE-KEEPING

Bees have the reputation of being indefatigable and industrious workers with a well-organized and economical home-life. They also produce honey, and it is for this happy reason that bees have been wooed and cultivated over thousands of years. Ken B has kept bees since he left the R.A.F. after the last war. He started off with one hive and gradually built up to ten hives, and then up to sixty hives. At that point, nine years ago, bee-keeping became more than a hobby; he, his wife and youngest daughter moved to a caravan in a Kent orchard with one hundred hives while they built a house and outbuildings. That was a good year for honey and they ended up extracting two tons of honey by hand under the light of a Tilly lamp. Once the honey was in twenty-eight pound tins they looked around for buyers. Nobody wanted twenty-eight pound tins. So Audrey B loaded up the car with one pound jars of honey and took it straight to the shops.

So they have continued, building up the stocks to 250 colonies of bees, building up knowledge and equipment and building a barn when the garage became too small. Now they have quite an establishment and last year, at fifty-one, Ken B retired from the dockyard to devote himself full-time to bees. What is it about bees that attracts him? 'You've never finished learning,' he says. 'No matter how long you've been bee-keeping you don't know all the answers. When I look at a colony of bees it's like being a super-detective, all the signs are there. You've got to go with the bees, never try to work against them. You move a colony from apples to pears but if they want to work bluebells they'll work bluebells. If they want to swarm it's better to take a nucleus off them or change the queen rather than going bullheaded and saying, "You're not going to swarm," because they will.'

Ken B keeps about twenty to twenty-five hives in each apiary which he farms out around the near-by orchards, fields and woodlands. He first takes the bees out to cherry around April 15th and then goes from orchard to orchard as the trees come into blossom. Farmers pay him £7.50 a hive during the fruit pollination period of a week or two. When they come back from the orchards about half the bees go out on to fields of beans; then for the rest of the summer they rely mainly on flowers and weeds in the district. The honey yield is dependent on the weather. Cold, wet weather is the worst; a season which warms up slowly and surely is the best. Everything the bees produce can be used – from honey to wax to propolis, a sticky substance used for making antibiotics.

Audrey B helps Ken on his rounds of the hives. 'When we come to an apiary,' he says, 'the wife gets her book out and reads out the history of each hive as we come to it, which helps when I am diagnosing its present condition. She gives the bees a puff of smoke and she writes down my assessment of that hive in her book. Anything I do, like change the queen, or if the hive needs a new roof, all that goes in the book.' Besides essential on-site work, Audrey B is a valuable pair of hands at extracting time. She also helps mend bee equipment, does the accounts, writes letters, bottles the honey, delivers it and collects the money.

With 250 hives increasing to 400 it is a full-time occupation for two people, at least during the summer months. The hours are also irregular. 'Sometimes in the summer we're up at four or five in the morning and then have nothing to do until ten or eleven at night, when the bees go to bed and we can move them.' This 'unsociability' is one reason why bee-keeping is such an individual business. Another reason is that there is no one way of managing bees; several different ways may be more or less successful according to environment and local conditions. Ken B advises: 'You don't start by saying you want to be a bee farmer. You start by having a few bees and building up your knowledge. Then you'll know whether you can make a living from it.'

Six months later

'I think there's a great future in commercial bee-keeping,' says Ken B, 'but bee-keepers have got to get mechanized.' Mechanized? 'Yes, there are small machines that will help you on your way, will do all the heavy work and the lifting which wears bee-keepers out. You have to see what you want and adapt it to suit yourself. For example, I've just bought a second-hand bottling machine this season.'

Part-time as a hobby

Capital: one hive, bees, equipment, extractor, clothing about £100
couple of hives could be kept in suburban garden; more hives need more land (see above), transport (landrover or equivalent) and separate extracting and bottling shed

Income: one hive produces fifty to one hundred pounds of

honey sold around 50p wholesale price
Qualifications: none

RIDING STABLES

Tricia G has worked with horses since she left school. Now, with her husband and four children, she is running her own stables in the Forest of Dean. They decided to move six years ago and found a small farmhouse with outbuildings and eighteen acres of land not too far off the beaten track. It took nearly all their money to get it and, hardly had the ink dried on the contract, she was out buying her first ponies. 'It was bewildering at first,' she says, 'because I had never bought horses before, but people were very helpful and took us to markets.' She soon discovered that 'there's luck as well as good judgment in buying horses; with a car a mechanic can tell you if it's right or not, but with a horse there's the temperament as well.'

The school was open as soon as the first two ponies arrived; more ponies followed and business snowballed. 'In retrospect,' she says, 'we were in too much of a hurry, everything cost us the limit. Living in the town you go to a shop and buy something; you don't realize that if you sit and listen to people it's amazing what they come up with.' One of the initial hurdles was getting planning permission and a licence from the council, 'from people who don't know anything about horses. It sounds all right in theory but isn't sensible in practice. I had to have a fire axe which I can't even lift.'

Eighteen horses and eighteen acres is as much as Tricia G can manage. She has one assistant and invaluable part-time help from her husband, who does most of the heavy work with the tractor and repairs the buildings. Half the ponies are regularly giving lessons and rides at weekends throughout the year and trekking six days a week in the summer. There is no lack of demand from children wanting to ride and over the years Tricia G has also established block bookings from local schools and P.G.L. Children's Holidays.

The trekking ponies subsidize the other half of her work: breaking and schooling young or badly trained horses, keeping a couple of hunter liveries and breeding. Like many other people working with horses Tricia G enjoys this best, but like many others she finds that the financial return is small. Even with the working ponies it is not easy to make the stables pay. She now charges £1.50 an hour for riding, which is double the original 75p; on the other hand, the cost of keeping horses has more than doubled. 'At least three or four places have started up round here,' she says, 'and have closed down. I think it's because they've sunk too much money in it and expected too much back from it.' Hay is one of the largest expenses and, of course, the horses must be fed even if they are not paying for their keep at that time. 'If we hadn't got the winter riding', she says, 'to keep us ticking over, we would have to sell everything at the end of each summer. P.G.L. would like us to do more trekking, so we wonder whether it's worthwhile to expand for the summer and close down more in the winter so I can do more schooling and breaking.'

This question of whether to expand or not has come up once before, after the stables had been going for three years. 'At that time,' she says, 'we had a sort out to keep things on the level, but it's difficult to keep a business at a certain size. If you want to make a living you have to cater for the demand to keep the place going. We could do four times as much work but we would be so busy, taking on more and more staff, that we would not get any pleasure out of it. So we're trying to improve the facilities we have rather than expand.'

How much experience do you need before starting a stables? 'Lots,' she says. 'You need to have worked in a stables before. Looking after your own pony at home isn't enough, you need to be able to manage thirty. It's seeing the dangers as well. I'm very safety-conscious, I never believe anybody when they say they can ride; they have to go out on slow, quiet rides. And we never use ponies under five or six for trekking; they have to be absolutely reliable. Another thing about working with lots of horses is that you learn how to cut the vet's bills with preventative medicine. You have to know what you can treat and when you call the vet.'

'Really,' she adds, 'it's all making do, which can be fun.'

Six months later
'Everything is very much the same,' says Tricia G. '. . . The tack room has been built.'

Full-time
Capital: £12,000 for house and eighteen acres
one pony costs between £50 and £150
hay is £60 to £100 a ton; Tricia G needs eighteen to twenty tons a year
horsebox is useful but not essential; costs £500
student assistant costs £7 to £10 a week
family assistance
Income: A
Qualifications: British Horse Society examinations
employment in riding stables

Chapter Two
Paper & Pictures

GRAPHIC DESIGN

Like many another ex-art student Caroline P, a graphic designer and illustrator, wanted to work freelance. She initially gained experience in advertising agencies, one job following another until, about three years ago, she said to herself, 'Right, this is it' – and left work. 'Then, panic, all the contacts I had made fell through, every one of them.' She started from the beginning. 'I had a folio, that's very important, things that have been published or highly finished roughs. I started going round, ringing up every art buyer in all the advertising agencies, just names to me. The trouble is they see hundreds of people every week, but I got a couple of jobs and slowly it picked up. I was on the dole at the time and doing one day's teaching a week, otherwise I wouldn't have been able to survive.'

Caroline P works mainly for agencies; she does both design and illustration, sometimes one-off jobs, sometimes a string of work. It's well-paid work if you can get it. 'You can never sit back and wait for more work to come through,' she says. 'Work places dry up. I may do a couple of months' work and then I'm back to taking my folio round again.' Timing is also important. 'Agencies want work very quickly; you have to work all night if necessary and it can be very disturbing. Publishing is easier in this respect. I'm designing a play pack which is two weeks' work, but I won't have to give it in for several months.'

Graphic design, like some other freelance work, can be a doleful business without considerable reserves of willpower. 'I work alone,' says Caroline P, 'and you have to learn to understand yourself and discipline yourself and not go under when you feel gloomy. When I haven't got work it's depressing, and I go out and see people and that's tiring and I come back and the phone doesn't ring and I should be sitting down and producing something good for my folio. This still isn't easy for me, but you have to come to terms with it.' Negotiating money also needs steely nerves. 'On a budget they ask you whether you can do the work for this amount. That's either yes or no. The other way is, "How much do you want for this job?" and it's a test to see how much you can get without going too far.'

Caroline P has never had an agent in London, but she does have one in Paris whom she found by a couple of fortuitous phone calls when on holiday there. 'I thought, "That's the last I'll hear of that," but they gave me work a fortnight after I got back.' English illustration, says Caroline, has a good reputation abroad and, since it pays well, it is worth establishing an agent if at all possible. Agent or no, Caroline P's freelance life has progressed fairly steadily, with the usual ups and downs, although one event nearly unseated her. She was about to go into partnership with a small typographical and window blind company. At the last minute the other partners changed their minds. 'The moral of that tale', she says, 'is that before going into something new get everything written, signed and sealed before you stop doing what brings in the bread and butter. Carry on as if it's not happening until everything is settled. It isn't just me, I've met other people to whom the same thing happened.'

Robin A and his partner have just gone into business designing posters, sleeves and booklets for the record industry. Robin A is a graphic designer who has taught for several years at St Martins and Norwich art schools; he is doing most of the designing while his partner, an ex-art director, goes out and gets work. It is a balanced partnership, each complementing the other, but to find it Robin A had to give up his four days a week teaching. 'I was doing too much teaching and not enough freelance,' he says, 'so my usefulness to students was becoming less and less.' He cut his teaching down to a day and a half and worked at home; now the business is moving into an office where it can provide a complete service, commissioning photographers and illustrators where necessary. 'We are prepared to take the job right through to the end, to take the whole onus of that responsibility away from the client. As a result of doing small and mundane things clients have realized we can carry them off. Now they give us a bigger job and expect to see it completed in an allotted amount of time.'

This capacity for accepting responsibility and working under pressure takes some time to develop. It is not something which the art schools can teach students. 'There's no way the art schools can recreate the demands of the commercial world,' says Robin A. 'We can tell students but they won't really know. The deadlines we impose on students are purely arbitrary. In order to get first-hand experience of what it is like to work outside everyone should get a job for eight months to a year when they leave college, just so they know how different it is. Otherwise it will be difficult to produce a service which is watertight.'

Isn't it a risky commitment starting a business at this time? 'My partner had no option,' he says, 'he had left his job. I am in a safer position, having teaching; fortunately the record industry is not affected to the same extent as some other industries by economic gloom. We have put all our eggs into one basket because we have to convince people that we can do whatever they want us to. Once we get that established we can look round for work of a different nature – such as publishing.'

What about working out of London? 'There's not usually so much scope but there are pockets, such as Norwich, where you can set yourself up with a steady supply of work. The kind of work you get depends on the area. Norfolk, for example, is a light industry and agricultural area and that governs the graphics that's required.'

Eight months later
Caroline P is looking for an agent in London. When she finds one she will have more time to 'start various little ventures. I don't really want to say too much in case they don't happen but one of these will be designing and printing a herb chart – what herbs go with what food – and selling it to shops, and another one will be printing patterns on china.'

Full-time
Capital: none
no separate premises
Income: B
Qualifications: five years Epsom Art College
employment

Nine months later
'The business is going well,' says Robin A. 'We had a slack period in the summer but it's picked up again now. We've had a problem getting money out of one client. In the end we had to say that we won't do any more record sleeves for them until they paid up. We've also been blackmailed into joining the National Graphical Association because they now won't accept pasted-up ads from non-union members.'

Part-time (3½ days)
Capital: sufficient for drawing boards, typewriter, cassette tape recorder, Polaroid camera and usual office equipment – from £100 to £500 (from shoestring to well-equipped). A good drawing board costs

£200. Robin A and partner are sponsored by another company
Income: B/C
Qualifications: Dundee Art College and Royal College of Art
teaching and freelance work

TYPESETTING

Jean W's one-room office is up several flights of stairs in Covent Garden. It is dominated by a large IBM typesetter, planted on a sturdy desk and flanked by rows of golf-balls for changing the typeface. IBM typesetting is a comparatively modern process. It shouldered its way into the printing world when offset printing largely replaced letterpress for small, cheap, quick jobs. A typesetter may look like a glorified typewriter, but it is capable of producing type which can be run off into books, magazines, newspapers, anything printed.

Jean W has been working on her own for nearly two years. She started off with little more than £500 and, on her own admission, a pair of very wobbly knees. Her business continued on faith rather than large receipts and it is only in the last three or four months that she has begun to draw a proper salary. She reckons to invoice £20 a day which has to cover £100 a month rent for the typesetter, £20 a week for rent, gas and electricity and her initial expenses such as golf-balls which set her back £600 in the first year.

Despite the comparatively high outgoings, Jean W works in central London because 'all my work is here, people knocking on my door with a couple of hours' work which I do within one or two days. I know a plate maker and I do the majority of his work which occupies me about two days a week, all small jobs. Then I do the autumn and spring promotional work for a publisher. The rest is other small jobs. I work quite late sometimes because I know that my business depends on a quick turnover.' There has never been any lack of work. 'You want people to recommend you to others; a good name is worth any amount of advertising. I have only had two spells without work and that only lasted about two hours.' The business takes up most of Jean W's time. 'I'm really surprised at the long hours I work,' she says, 'really for self-esteem and the satisfaction of making a go of it. It's nothing to do with money; my salary is half what I would earn if I had a job.'

It was a big step for Jean W to work for herself after nearly twenty years as a typesetter. On one or two previous occasions she considered setting up on her own, but hesitated until a friend started a typesetting business and she began taking the overspill. 'That first six months,' she says, 'you're frightened all the time that you're not going to make it and then one morning you wake up and realize that it's a success.' There were any number of things to learn: how much to charge, for instance. 'I decided on £3 an hour and more for complicated work. I've never kept an accurate account of how many hours I work. I'm sure that if I charge £4 an hour for four hours work it's taken me five hours by the time I've done this and that.' Time-keeping can be a bit of a problem. 'I do waste time in that I'll go out and see customers and on the way back wander round the shops. Today I've had an unsuccessful day taking time up with phone calls and I'll have to make it up tomorrow.'

Although Jean W deliberately chooses small jobs, there are other kinds of typesetting work. 'The big, continuous work is more profitable,' she says, 'because you sit down and work for six hours. My friend in the country does books because she has a two-machine unit which eats up texts. Her work is different to mine; her work is large-volume work where her rates are lower because she's out in the suburbs.' There is typesetting work all over the country but 'the closer you are to a printer the more work you will get. No matter what you do it's got to be printed. You might do work for a large company which prints internally or typeset a society's newsletters or bulletins. If you had a regular source of work you could sit at home in the Isle of Man.'

Jean W learnt typesetting almost as an apprentice to an agency and it is second nature to her now. Is it an easy skill to learn? 'Anybody can type on one of those IBM machines; it's very efficient and IBM have swamped the market. If you buy one they give the operator a three-day course. They tell you which buttons to press but they don't tell you why you do it. It's really experience and interest that takes you out of being an ordinary typist to doing what the printer wants.'

Nine months later

'I've found myself getting very hard and distrustful,' says Jean W, 'because people are not paying me. I've become very disillusioned with human nature.' Do you get paid in the end? 'I haven't actually had any bad debts, but it sometimes takes months. I now make sure that I charge the right amount, no favours. Perhaps it's as well, I was far too soft and pliable before.'

Full-time

Capital: £500 (£200 own money, £300 borrowed)
largest expense is £115 a month for hire of typesetter (no longer £100)
separate premises

Income: A ('because I've been paying for my capital expenditure this year')

Qualifications: fifteen years' typesetting experience

TRANSLATING

Françoise W is French and married to an Englishman. She works from home translating English business, engineering or industrial reports, briefs and transactions into her native language. It is not enough, as she quickly pointed out, to be fluent in another language. She has to know the technical or specialist terms common to any engineering or building business and to be able to apply them in any context. The same goes for most business translating. It all sounds quite formidable, is it? 'You should be employed as a translator,' she recommends, 'before starting freelance, since most translating is business translating. That way you get to know the terminology, what words are used and how they are used. Even now when I am working freelance I must read magazines and journals to keep up with current events and current inventions, just to know what is going on.'

Françoise W is registered with a translating agency and most of her work arrives with the postman. It may be a lot of work or nothing at all. Sometimes she gets a preliminary phone call. 'I enjoy it most of the time,' she says, 'but it can get very boring. You don't need to go out and see anybody. You don't know what happens to the work; you do it and send it back. It is almost too easy.'

There are other ways of working. A translator might work in a client's office for two or three days a week or even very occasionally. Françoise W started work with one company planning to be there for four weeks and stayed three months. That finished recently, or has it? 'They recruited one translator to go to Algeria and when he goes at the end of the month I might be called up again. I might never go back, I might go back, I just don't know. I have phoned them, they don't know either, it depends on the work load.' And the work load depends on the overseas contacts which British firms are making and the amount of written material which passes backwards and forwards between them. French is probably the most common language needed here, closely followed by German or Spanish. Even Arab contracts are usually in English or French. Fees reflect this. French, being most in demand, pays £7.75 per thousand words as set out by the Institute of Linguists. Other less commonly used languages pay more. Literary translation is costed along similar lines.

It might be unsettling not knowing what the morning's

post will bring or whether direct clients will supply work, but it is also flexible which suits Françoise W, a mother with two young children. 'My children are five and eight,' she says, 'and they still need me. If I don't say, "We will do this or that," they will be watching television all evening. I feel I have a role here, whereas in three or four years time they will be wanting to be more on their own and they won't need me so much. I might as well take advantage of these years when I am needed at home.' For some mothers, working at home may be the best way of combining care for a family with contributions to the budget. Françoise W does not have to rely on translating but, if she did, 'I would find new clients, direct clients that I would work for, not all the time, but quite regularly, following up a job, going back to it as I was needed, and learning from it.'

Although most commercial translating is carried out in London or other big cities, there is no intrinsic reason why translators should not live almost anywhere. 'Most of it arrives by post,' she says, 'and if you build up your clients, either direct or through an agency, and if you work at your subject through periodicals then you can translate in the country. After all, the postman goes everywhere.'

Seven months later
'I'm still freelance, but for the last six months I've been working full-time for a consulting engineering firm in Epsom. I've still got the agency but I'm not using it at all at the moment now that I'm permanently working. I could walk out tomorrow as I'm freelance, but it seems to be going on.'

Part-time originally, now full-time
Capital: none
no separate premises
Income: B, now C
Qualifications: native language French, fluent English
previous business employment

SECRETARIAL

As an actress Anne P needed a more secure income. She took a crash secretarial course and started work as a 'temp'. What immediately struck her was the variety of the work; it was quite a surprise. 'One week I was sitting in a private office with a beautiful carpet, an intercom and the vice-president of a company and the next week I was working for a charitable organization which was so narrow and tight in its outlook that I had to go to the roof or the ladies' loo for a smoke.' Adaptability might be the hallmark of a good temp, she feels. She also feels that secretarial work is very often underrated and undervalued because 'anybody can learn to do shorthand and typing and that can be the end of the job. A good secretary offers a more complete service, takes an interest in the work. The lack of this service is one reason why secretarial work has got a bad name both from the standard of work that is given and from the way employers treat staff.'

One job led to another, at first for her husband and then, after a period of employment, working freelance. The simplest way of getting work is to go to an agency; there is one in every high street. 'My immediate reaction was to go to one of the big chains of agencies but then I saw an advertisement for a small local agency. It suits me very well because it's geared to the needs of its secretaries as well as its other clients.'

So the agency one picks is important? 'Depending on what you want to do. Medical secretaries are an obvious specialized case. The agency I work for caters for people who are either at home with children (provided that work can be collected and returned) or a mother without a husband to support her – so they put work her way.' Experience helps, but 'I don't think you need to have worked in different fields. If you have kept your eyes open you can apply knowledge you had no idea would ever come in useful.

I have wrestled with an income tax form like most people. At the moment I'm working with an accountant and when he talks about "notice of assessment" or "capital gains tax" they're not entirely foreign terms to me.'

At one time there was so much demand for secretaries that agencies sprang up like mushrooms. In more stringent times there is still work, but the boom is over. 'I think you've got to initially accept what is offered to you and show willing to the agency. In the last three months since I started I have been extremely busy, even though November is reckoned to be a bad time. I think if you do good work it is recognized and people ask for you again. There is a subtle balance of letting the agency know you exist by going in once a week and never going near them. You need to keep the freshness of the contact without making them sick to death of you.'

Anne P has another interest, singing, and this is one of the reasons why she left her job and turned freelance. She squeezed a piano into her small flat and gives singing lessons at home. The agency work fits in well with other commitments. 'I have a certain amount of control over my time,' she says. 'The agency recognizes that some people may have careers which aren't self-supporting and they are prepared to give you back-up work.'

There are other ways of finding work besides going through an agency, such as advertising in the local paper, but 'at least working through an agency you're sure of getting paid.' One type of work to avoid is typing envelopes or mailing lists at home. It can pay as little as 85p an hour. The more usual secretarial rate is around and about £1.30. Although Anne P relies on the agency for work, 'if you're self-employed you do have to set up the business side in a small way. I've thought of getting some cards printed with name, address, telephone number and stating that one offered a fully comprehensive secretarial service. I would keep a pocketful with me constantly and offer them to people – get recommendations that way.'

Ten months later
'I'm just starting a new job tomorrow,' says Anne P. Why did she give up working freelance? 'I felt I didn't have enough commitment to the work outside a full-time job,' she says. 'All the same, working freelance gave me the opportunity of practising other skills, administrative skills, which I shall be using in my new job.'

Full-time
Capital: none; electric typewriter useful
no separate premises
Income: B
Qualifications: six-month secretarial course

EDITORIAL RESEARCH

Like most research, this is detective work: finding pictures and background information for use in books, magazines, documentaries and advertising. There are well-known sources of pictures but it can mean hunting down photographs in the most unlikely places, a job which is largely hard work with the occasional revelation.

There is no one recognized method of becoming a researcher. Angela M arrived at it in the most haphazard way. She got advice from a fellow researcher and then 'I told everybody I knew that I wanted to be a picture researcher and a couple of people came up with a couple of jobs.' Along the way she acquired a flat full of reference books, a telephone and typewriter, the tools of her trade.

Angela M has been a researcher for four years. Her first job was researching into 1930s cinemas for a documentary. Did she know anything about 1930s cinemas? 'Not to start with. I just got all the books on cinema, I joined the Cinema Theatre Association, spoke to the Historic Buildings Commission. This was just factual research. I did take some photographs but the idea was to find out about them, where they were, who built them and what they looked like.' If specialized knowledge is not needed then tenacity, resourcefulness and an ability to judge each picture on its merits is vital. A book of eighteenth-century ballads followed from Penguin Education and Angela M was asked to find Victorian and Edwardian photographs to illustrate it. She went all over England, to museums, libraries and collections of photographs. After nine months of working with Penguin, she knew her business. 'Most researchers have been employed before turning freelance but it's not essential and, touch wood, I have never been out of work.' Through another researcher she got a job working on a biography of Kate Greenaway. 'There is another biography written in 1906 and I had to find out if it was accurate. I found out where she lived from street directories, looked at old maps and read letters in the Public Records Office.' The book never crystallized.

About eighteen months ago publishers started cutting their lists, especially expensive books with pictures. This is one of the perennial problems, ensuring a supply of work, since the amount available depends on whether publishers and others are expanding or retracting. 'In some ways, though,' she says, 'it works better for freelancers since publishers may have got rid of staff and use freelancers for each particular job.' It also helps to be able to turn a hand to anything. In her time as a researcher Angela M has worked for a weekly psychology publication, the *New Scientist* and B.B.C. Publications and has found pictures and written copy for promotional wrap-arounds for Summer County Margarine ('on birds, animals, butterflies and places to go in the country').

There is little security in it. A job could be finishing one week and there's no knowing whether something will turn up for the next. But the phone goes and 'you go along to see the editor and he gives you a manuscript. At this stage a good picture researcher could save an editor a lot of time and money by advising on such things as reproduction rights and fees. He will either want something specifically or he tells you something like, "I want this many pictures, so many colour, so many black and white," and he might tell you what he doesn't want like engravings. Then you take the manuscript home and make a picture list and decide what the main subjects and people are. When you have a picture list you get books on the subject. You get an idea of the main sources and, since you know about them, everybody else knows about them, some pictures turn up time and again. Some of them will be there because they're the only pictures available. The editor also tells you what the budget is and if it's small you only have time to get in well-known pictures. Otherwise you hunt around and see what you can dig up.'

The digging up is a large part of a researcher's skill. The basic picture sources can be found in a number of handbooks but there are always new out-of-the-way sources to be discovered. One last question: does a researcher have to live in London? 'I think you probably do, or at least near a big city with advertising or publishing work and near sources of pictures. It's probably not work, except occasionally, for someone in the country.'

Nine months later
'I've just finished a six-month stint at the B.B.C.,' says Angela M, 'researching pictures for *The Age of Uncertainty*. It's by J.K. Galbraith and it's going to be shown in January. Now I'm doing bits and pieces; there might be a bigger project coming up soon. I think you ought to say there isn't that much work available at the moment unless you're very well organized.'

Full-time
Capital: none
desk and typewriter essential
reference books around £50 (useful but not essential)
Income: B/C
Qualifications: none

PHOTOGRAPHY

Photography can be all things to all photographers: for some it is taking fuzzy pictures of the family, for others it is portraits or weddings, fashion or interiors, landscapes or photo-journalism for publishers of magazines, books or newspapers, travel agents, industry, architects and individuals. It is both highly technical and surrounded by an aura of art.

Anybody can press a button, but where do the good photographers come from? There is no educational slipstream to success. Colleges can teach techniques but not that flash of intuition; an assistant to an established photographer could learn more. Others fall in love with their first camera and carry on loving. John M began taking pictures when he was fifteen and then, in his first job with a diamond company, was called in to photograph their products. That decided him; he worked in darkrooms developing other people's work and, in his spare time, branched into colour photography, taking pictures for Candlemakers Supplies. It was all very gradual – developing skills, building up experience and slide collections – until a year ago when his job came to an end. He went freelance.

If John M's photographic education was home-grown, then Sam S's was a fluke. After a heart attack at twenty-eight he convalesced over a Box Brownie and a darkroom in the garage, following instructions in books as he went. If he needed to know about colour he got another book. John Makepeace, the furniture designer, was his first regular client. Other work followed, leading to a job with Marks and Spencers to photograph a fashion Dickens centenary year. It was all heart in mouth to begin with, but it won him an award and other work came along; most of it is fashion and interiors.

Sam S is fortunate in that he has another career (see p.45) and another income. For John M, with a wife and child, it was quite a plunge. 'You can't count on anything,' he says.

'I had some capital to start with but after this year I shall have to pay my way.' Soon after he began on his own, Search Press asked him to photograph crafts for a series of books; he is on the fourth book. Meanwhile, he takes pictures of Norfolk and Cornwall and pictures of children. What can be done with these? 'I send them away to magazines – I've got some in photographic magazines in Australia – or I can send them to an agency. In either case they might sit on them for a year or so and even then not publish them. Really, it all goes back to foot-slogging around with a portfolio, finding out about the market, who to go to. For example, there's not a good stock of pictures of farm animals – not much good for me, I don't live in the country, but that's the sort of thing worth knowing about.'

Marketing pictures can eat up more time than taking them. 'I might be working two days a week,' says John M, 'and then I've got to go backwards and forwards. I'm seeing my publisher today; it will take me an hour there, an hour back and two hours talking. It all takes time.'

It also takes money. John M's work is largely small-scale tabletop photography in his own home. It is an expensive business, though, to finance a studio. Sam S speaks from experience. 'If you have a studio you need at least five hundred square feet including a darkroom. Even if you share a studio with somebody you're talking about a minimum of £20 a week outgoings and £6,000 investment in equipment and transport. Now you either buy equipment and organize yourself, which costs money, or you can be a man with a camera who sets himself up with £100 to £1,000. In that case you're competing with all the amateurs or ex-art students who also have cameras.'

Nine months later

'I'm working two or three days a week for Candlemakers Supplies,' says John M. 'I have a studio there and I can use it for other work as well.'

Full-time
Capital: camera cost £200
darkroom equipment cost £50
use of studio
Income: B
Qualifications: none

Eight months later
'The photography business is continuing quite well,' says Sam S. 'It's hard times for everybody at the moment. The thing to remember for anybody starting up is don't skimp on equipment, keep overheads low and don't borrow money.'

Part-time
Capital: equipment is usually imported so prices have shot up
35 mill camera system from £1,100
enlarger £600 plus lenses from £8 to £200
electronic flash system from £500 plus heads
equipment for studio £1,100
studio fittings £200
electricity fittings £100
glazer £100
drier £40
studio 450 square feet minimum
transport essential to carry equipment
Income: C
Qualifications: none

COMPUTER PROGRAMMING

Alan F had been up all night with one of his favourite occupations: computer programming. He packs in forty or fifty hours a week working freelance on a computer system for a tobacco importers. Computer science is an absorbing and challenging discipline with its own language and methodology: absorbing for its adherents, mystifying to outsiders.

'There are basically two types of programming,' says Alan F, 'scientific and commercial. The commercial is mainly payrolls and stocks, money and units. A computer can arrange data such as orders and invoices, it can maintain files and provide material for long-term analysis and it can prepare reports for management. In other words, it can deal with all the needs and requirements of the company. For example, two typists could type out labels to go on orders. The computer could do the orders and as a spin-off print the labels in three or four minutes.' In scientific programming, on the other hand, 'you're dealing with fractional parts. Engineering formulae, for example, may have great strings of variables, amazing calculations; you may need to find the square root of something to a really accurate figure. In commercial programming these things aren't done, you don't need to find the square root of anyone's payroll.'

A lot of people working with computers are young, 'they've just come out of university a couple of years, everything is new in the business. Someone can work on a project for a year and find something new and it's been staring him in the face all the time.' Alan F did not go to university, he got a job with London University Computing Services in 1972. 'I was lucky, I had done maths and a bit of statistics and computer science and I was put under the guidance of a whiz-kid statistician economist who showed me systems work. I learnt as I went along.' Could anybody walk into a job like that? 'No, especially now, there's been a recession in big, centralized computers which have become uneconomic except for specific tasks. Work is still available, though. There are lots of ads in papers offering so many thousands after so many months' training. Watch out for some of these ads; they could be agencies with bogus jobs.' It is also city work. 'All the computers are in Bristol, London, Birmingham, Manchester, places like that; there aren't any in the countryside, you don't need a computer to plough a field.'

After two years Alan F had worked on statistics, compiling

and graphics and thought he had learned as much as he needed. He tried one job in Hanover and then another with a small company working on mini computers. It was commercial work on a shoe-string budget. When the company could no longer afford to keep him he went freelance. 'It's always something that programmers bear in mind,' he says. 'You may have experience in a particular field which isn't needed by one company full-time, you would be wasted, but they may need you for one month a year. The work is there if you've got experience. You might be employed on a part-time basis but what they'll more likely want is some months' continuous work from you.'

In the near future hardware (computers) are going to drop dramatically in price rather like the pocket calculator. This opens up a number of possibilities: one, that hardware manufacturers, finding their profits low on hardware, start selling ready-made software (programmes) thus cutting out the freelance programmer, and two, that more, cheaper computers will generate experiment and invention and the employment of freelancers. All sorts of things could happen – it's that kind of market – but, nevertheless, the more common your skills the easier it is to get work. Specialized skills and experience with rare machines are more difficult to transfer. 'If you go to a new machine,' says Alan F, 'you can use fifty per cent of what you already knew. The rest has to be learned.'

Freelance work is a mixed blessing for some. 'It has headaches and advantages,' he says. 'Firstly, will you be able to get enough work, sell enough of your time; secondly, you have to deal with tax, be meticulous about handling books. The advantages are working only when the work is there. I don't like to be in a job where I'm not used.' Besides invoices and time sheets he keeps a record of useful contacts and conversations about work. Charges are set out at £2.50 an hour, £2 minimum, £3 possible. 'Usually people like to pay out by the hour because it's more important to get everything right than to save a bit on time.'

Seven months later
'I'm still working freelance for the tobacco importers,' says Alan F. 'The future is hazy but the system I'm working on has become comprehensive and saleable. If it takes off I would be employed by a number of companies, including one with fifty warehouse branches. We've already had demonstrations for interested parties.'

Full-time
Capital: none
no separate premises
Income: C
Qualifications: relevant A levels
previous employment

BOOK-KEEPING

Michael K has fingers in several pies, all to do with money, but his bread and butter pie is a book-keeping service for other self-employed people and small businesses. It was never intended to be that way. He was a banker with London and County Securities which folded in 1973, leaving Michael K on the street with a living to earn. He tried financial consultancy which worked quite well until the economic situation got worse and then he tried doing company searches (which he still does); now he has added book-keeping to his other activities and in a couple of weeks he starts a computerized payroll.

Book-keeping first: it's work for individuals or small companies, architects, designers, builders and so on, collecting the invoices once a month and writing up the books. Very often V.A.T. demands precipitate a call for help. Michael K advertises for clients and they answer the ads at the rate of about four a month. About a quarter are one-off jobs and the rest continue. 'A lot of people say, "I'm two years behind." So you get them up to date and they say, "Fine, I can see how it's done, it's easy," which it is, so they do it themselves. Others say, "You've got it up to date, fine, keep on coming because we don't want the hassle of knowing about it." I've just come here straight from a new client. He has a neurosis about opening bank statements and income tax forms. There was a bundle of envelopes – about thirty bank statements, four letters from the tax man and the renewal of his wife's motor car licence. All he wants is for me to go round once a month, open any brown envelopes, say how much he has earned, how much money he owes and who he should pay.' This anxiety about brown envelopes is not that unusual, apparently. 'Some people don't understand money, don't want to know, close their eyes to it,' he says.

Most of Michael K's work is straightforward book-keeping. 'Anybody who can write up books can provide a book-keeping service. You might not produce a set of accounts, but in nine cases out of ten they don't need a set of accounts. Fundamentally, all any small business needs to know on the financial side is how much money does it owe and how much is it owed, because the difference between these is solvency and non-solvency.'

For one firm of architects Michael K does a monthly analysis of hours spent on each project to help the firm invoice clients. He also provides a cash flow forecast so the firm can go to the bank and say, 'This is how money is going to come in and go out over the next year. We need X number of pounds for these peak periods. On the basis of the cash flow we can repay it within a year.' That is a bit more than book-keeping, isn't it? 'Yes, even small companies sometimes need financial advice but could not employ somebody with my skills and experience; they could, and should, afford to employ somebody on a part-time basis, once a month, or every three months.' Arranging fees, says Michael K, is a matter of 'sticking a finger out of the window and seeing which way the wind is blowing. It varies between £40 and £60 a month according to how much work I think is involved. From some people we get more than it is worth because they would rather pay £50 a month and not know about it. One guy, though, he hasn't got much money and I charge about half of what it is worth. It's swings and roundabouts.'

Michael K works in a loose association with other people providing a range of services from business and financial management to artwork and design. Besides book-keeping he contributes another line of work, a company investigation service. 'If anybody wants to know about a limited company,' he says, 'we do searches and give information.' It costs about a fiver and involves half an hour of his time at Companies House. 'We wrote to literally hundreds of solicitors and got three replies. But we get enough business. What we try and provide is a fantastically fast service, a forty-eight hour turnround. We can get information that day which a normal search agency wouldn't do. We can also get technical information which a run-of-the-mill person from an agency would miss.'

The third leg of Michael K's business is going to be the payroll service. Many companies organize their wages and salaries through computer bureaux but most bureaux, he says, are not interested if you have less than two hundred employees. 'If I can get a dozen small companies together, we're big enough for a bureau. I deal with the computer wholesale and retail it out to my clients.' All sorts of analyses can be done. 'If you are doing a purchase ledger for a factory you might want an analysis of raw materials, services, wages; then you might want all these things broken down by departments. It's like keeping a set of books: you have wages in one column, national insurance in another, electricity, rates, rent and the rest. What I can do is provide that analysis for six different people all at the same time. The computer looks on me as one client with six different departments.'

Seven months later
'After three and a half years,' says Michael K, 'Customs and Excise expect people to understand V.A.T. and are getting much tougher with those who do (or will) not.' As a consequence his book-keeping business is booming and he is considering whether to employ somebody to help with the work. The computer payroll service is not in operation because he has been so busy, but 'it could be set up tomorrow if somebody wanted it.' He has also started advertising in *The Times* and *Sunday Times.*

Full-time
Capital: for running an office (shared premises)
pocket calculator only piece of equipment 'apart from pen, pencil, ruler, rubber'
secretary costs £2,500 to £3,000 in London
Income: C
Qualifications: Associate Institute of Bankers (examinations include book-keeping and accountancy)

MARKET RESEARCH

All over the country market research interviewers are sitting down with 'members of the public', questionnaire in hand, inviting their views about any product from cosmetics to banking, from government policies to children's road safety. Elizabeth K has been an interviewer on and off for several years. A prime qualification for the job is a ready interest in people. 'If you are interested in the people you meet,' she says, 'not only because you want to interview them, they will find it easier to talk to you. Explain what the survey is about, not just to sell X bars of soap but to get a better product, to help themselves in a way.'

This is part-time freelance work which fits in well with other commitments: children at school or husband away on work. Market research is usually carried out by married women with families rather than men or young girls. 'The reason for this is obvious,' she says. 'If a strange man came to the door, especially if it was the door of a little old lady, many women wouldn't answer and they might resent a young woman. It's simple for them if you're not at all frightening.'

The surveys are organized by market research companies employing regional controllers; their job is to co-ordinate local interviewers recruited from advertisements in such newspapers as the *Daily Telegraph* or *Evening Standard.* Flexibility is the key note here. After a short period of training interviewers select available dates from an advance calendar; they are subsequently briefed before a survey, sometimes at a conference, sometimes with written instructions. Then it's up to the interviewer how she organizes her working life. 'A quota of so many people is given, either selected by random sample or from the electoral roll. So you have to interview fifty people, for example, within ten days from June 12th to June 30th. You do it to suit yourself in your own time.'

Appointments are made, sometimes in the evening, and can take anything from a few minutes to an hour depending on the survey and how much the interviewee knows. Sometimes it's not very much. 'You would never put words into their mouths, but you would try and remind them by saying, "Surely you've read about it in the papers or seen it on television or heard somebody talking about it?" ' There is skill in conducting the interview. 'You have to try and get the person interested,' says Elizabeth K, 'so instead of saying "I don't know," they do know. You also have to judge whether people are telling the entire truth; sometimes they're not.'

It is essential to be an accurate recorder, especially with open-ended questions where every word must be written down as it is spoken. 'One man got very hot under the collar and every other word was a four-letter one. I had to write down every single one, some of them I hadn't heard of. Really, you have to be prepared for anything. A mother might be changing a baby's nappy, the front door bell goes and you're left holding the baby. Sometimes you go in pretty grim houses and slightly tricky situations and then you either call back another day or cope with it as best you can.'

Although working times are flexible it can be concentrated work, driving and talking all day and writing up notes in the evening. An interviewer is very much on her own even though the company organizes and oversees the survey. On cold, wet days it must be a temptation to sit at home in front of the fire and fill in the answers. 'Yes,' says Elizabeth K, 'but you must never fill in the answer to a question, ever. That's one of the cardinal rules. Every now and again the regional controller goes back to a house which you have visited and checks that everything is as it should be. The company relies on you, it has to.' And pay? Normally pay is by the hour or the day plus certain expenses, such as petrol and fares, and should not be less than £1 an hour.

Six months later
Elizabeth K is no longer interviewing 'because it became very tiring'; instead she works part-time in a clothes shop.

Part-time
Capital: none
car essential for rural areas
Income: A
Qualifications: none

TELEPHONE ANSWERING

'I've been ringing you all week and you're never in.' If you've heard that before, especially if you've lost work because of it, the phone needs answering. The answer might be a disembodied voice on a machine or it could be somebody like Meryl H who runs a telephone answering service. Her clients are one-man businesses, freelance actors, musicians or photographers, car hire firms, doctors, foreign companies, travel agents or anybody else who would like a secretary but can't afford one.

For Meryl H it has been touch and go since she started six years ago and the business is only now beginning to pay its way. 'It's difficult when you start,' she says, 'you need to undercut prices to get work yet you want to offer quality, be different from your competitors.' Many other telephone answering services just take messages; this one offers a secretarial service, a nightline and an accommodation address and deals with advertising campaigns. 'We run their concern over the telephone, quote prices, take bookings, send out brochures. For instance, we have a client who is a car hire company. Over the evenings and weekends we are them, we get the car and find the chauffeur.'

Meryl H started the telephone answering service at home with one client – a friend who ran a discotheque. When her first child started answering the phone, she took on a small office with a flat above. During the day she and her only employee run the office. During the evening and at weekends the three people in the flat above organize it between themselves and Meryl H dashes down if there is an emergency.

It takes a cool head to keep track of sixty clients' problems and requirements. 'It isn't easy', says Meryl H, 'to make sure that everybody remembers that every client is very important. Even the ones who don't pay any extra, we still hold instructions on them; they may be away for a week, they may ask us not to give any messages unless a code number is quoted, little things like that which are a constant headache to get right.' Most answering services run on a card index system, a card for each client and messages in pigeon-holes. Meryl H uses cardboard folders. 'In theory that should work,' she says. 'The problem is that people think they know a client so they don't bother to look at the latest instruction – it's human error really.' Are there any clients that she won't take? 'I've just thrown a prostitute off the books – not because I disapprove but (a) her clients ring exclusively at night; (b) if a man answers the phone they ring off and (c) they treat our girls as though they were call girls. We take up strong references for any dubious clients like people who call themselves night-time security.'

Prospective clients, working out the costs, need a number of calls to justify the service; for some it is two or three a day, for others it could be one a month. In either case it costs £5.50 a month for a simple office-time message service, £8.50 for a 24-hour service to £24 a month for a full telephone secretary service, but 'we're lucky if we've got many clients paying £24 a month.' On top of that a client has to pay the Post Office to refer calls, an answering set to do the same or even invest in a car radio-phone or pocket pager. It all adds up and a simple answering machine, taking messages, might be more economical. 'Yes,' says Meryl H, 'but not many people on our books could use an answering machine. Imagine that you're in import-export; somebody wants to deliver goods and they get an answering machine. They don't know if you're away for a fortnight or an hour. If they get us we can say, "We're expecting him back in half an hour," so they know they've made contact.'

Keeping the answering service in front of the public eye is part of the business. Clients come through the grapevine, the Yellow Pages and the occasional article in the press. Meryl H also produces a four-page folder advertising the service. If she had some spare money, 'I would spend it on promotion, letting the right newspapers, such as the *Financial Times*, know about us.' It has been hard work, not recommended to anybody without thorough market research beforehand or combining telephone answering with other work; Meryl H is hoping to find a partner and start an instant print section as an additional service.

Seven months later
'It's the telephone bills which are really hitting us,' says Meryl H. 'They've gone up from £200 – £300 two years ago to £2,000 – £3,000, and although we've got five more lines it's about the same number of calls. We had a drastic price rise four months ago from £8.50 to £12.50 for new clients. Old clients we look at individually to see if they can take it. The instant print is still very small as yet; it's intended for local businesses and our own clients.'

Part-time (sometimes full-time)
Capital: £100 at first (£30 on typewriter)
£2,000 later spent on equipping office, furnishing flat, telephone installation
rent of premises (including flat above) £1,250 a year
total employment bill £5,000 yearly (includes full-time assistant, part-time help and occasional contingency help)
instant print machine £1,300 (borrowed from mother)
Income: A
Qualifications: none

INDUSTRIAL DESIGN

Industrial design engineering has been Bill M's chosen career since the age of fourteen. Together with four other associates he designs mass-produced items, largely metal or plastics, and either consumer goods such as washing machines, phones and toasters or capital equipment like computers, electronic and optical instruments. The skill and expertise they command is quite formidable and requires many years training. Some of the problems they encounter, though, and ways of dealing with them, throw light on group consultancy work as a whole.

Most industrial design is carried out within a company,

but a significant proportion is consultancy work which brings the advantages of good design to small and middle size manufacturers. 'A group of five people is a fairly large chunk of pure industrial design,' says Bill M. 'It has to be a very big firm to have a department of designers like ours. That's the benefit of consultancy. You have experience in a wide range of fields, problems are common, techniques can be crossed over; for example, you can borrow a piece of electronics and put it in a consumer product.' The disadvantage of consultancy is obvious: the designer is not on the spot. One way of overcoming this weakness is to arrange an 'in house' service, the designer working in the company for, say, one day a week. 'You have to find out what the company is like,' says Bill M, 'remembering that it is a group of people not an arbitrary thing. They have certain aims, an attitude which is built up through the company's history, plant which is allowing them to produce things in certain ways. An individual working within the company gets to know all about these difficulties and restraints. Unless you find out about these unique aspects you are liable to do something which is not relevant for them'.

Most people, working for themselves, have to cross a couple of hurdles called 'getting paid' and 'getting work'. Getting paid isn't often a major problem; it's when you get paid that counts. Three months after the work is finished is not uncommon; Bill M may have started work two months before that. 'When you're starting on your own,' he says, 'you can't afford to do it full-time, you're almost bound to start part-time. You just need a couple of lucky breaks, which always come, to give you the first impetus. From then on it should be a firm growth.' The temptation is often to expand too fast without a firm base. 'The only rule of thumb is to keep it slow. Get the work first, then provide the facilities, rather than the other way round. It's an obvious commonsense thing.'

Keeping overheads low can mean solvency in a crisis.

Bill M and associates were badly hit by the three-day week. 'There are supposed to have been several industrial crises since I started six years ago but none of them affected us at all except that, and that affected us absolutely across the board. We had an overall turnover drop of forty per cent, a lapse for six months. There's an attitude in industry which considers an industrial designer slightly luxurious and firms will always cut their research and development before they cut lots of other things.' Work has picked up considerably since then, some of it abroad. 'The fall of the pound has made us very competitive,' says Bill M. 'We find that going to the continent – France, Denmark, Germany – we can afford to cover travelling costs on quite small jobs. I reckon we could work in the States if we got the clients. Americans are expensive because they organize everything on a three to one basis. If a man sets up on his own he sets up with a businessman and a salesman which makes him three times as expensive. With a business there is a point where it would be financially logical to carry promotional people, but once you do that you stop being able to design.'

Eight months later
'We are going on in very much the same direction,' says Bill M. 'Our work abroad has expanded considerably and now accounts for about seventy per cent of our turnover. There are now eight of us and we are planning to move into rented premises in the spring – that will bring all the overheads which we don't have at the moment.'

Full-time

Capital: about £300 to £400 per designer for drawing board, desk and draughting machine

no separate premises (top floor of house used as office; part of basement used as workshop)

part-time secretary for twenty hours a week at £2.50 an hour

Occupation: Self-Employed

Income: C
Qualifications: from Central School of Art and Design teaching, research and industrial experience

Chapter Three
Shops & Selling

MARKET STALLS

Nobody relishes standing in the freezing rain and wind for hours at a time and getting up before dawn for the privilege of doing so. Yet for many people market day in the elements gives them a living and often a good living at that. Sam S is one such person. He and his wife sell lace and trimmings, zips and buttons, cotton and threads at stalls in Banbury, Rugby, Market Harborough, Northampton, Oxford, Stratford on Avon and Portobello Road. It started off with £50 worth of peach embroidery.

At the age of twenty Sam S had made and lost a minor fortune with a restaurant and club and was looking for something else to do. His first pitch was in Portobello Road and that day he sold virtually all the peach embroidery. He carried on from there, first as a casual, 'a person who goes on if somebody else doesn't turn up', and then as a regular stallholder. 'In the week I got in fairly easily, but it took about five years to get a pitch on Portobello Road on a Saturday; in the country markets it took two to three years in most of them. In the first two years I was lucky to get on forty per cent of the time.'

Sam S buys his goods from wholesalers and direct from manufacturers. 'I buy a lot of job, clearing lines that manufacturers want to get rid of because they're the end of ranges. I used to spend all my time tearing around and buying; nowadays people ring me up. They say "We want £500," I say "I'll give you £350," we argue and I walk away with it for £400. We've had write-ups in local papers because our goods rival any main store in the country. I've recently bought fourteen thousand 1930s flowers which sell for £1.25 in the shops and we sell them for 25p. It's a very competitive business, there's always somebody ready to undercut you.'

Sam's wife, his partner, organizes and runs most of the stalls with the help of casual labour. Her working day starts with loading up the van – a ton and a half of zips, buttons etc. – driving to market, selling and reloading the van in the evening. She handles stock control, bundles everything except the lace (for ease of self-service) and keeps daily accounts. He supervises the stalls in London, buys stock, deals with financing and the payment of bills and V.A.T. – 'That's the most frightening thing for small businesses now; you not only have the pleasure of paying and of being an unpaid tax collector, but you have to work three days a quarter for the government just to keep it straight.'

It is not that easy to get a stall, especially in the fashionable markets. 'When I first started,' says Sam S, 'market traders were far less professional than they are now. Today they tend to be solid businesses with turnovers of £20,000 plus or hobbyists on a Saturday who don't really care whether they make any money or not because it's trendy to have a stall.' Small businesses are disappearing. 'The cost puts people off,' he says. 'Say you've got a stall at Rugby for the morning. It costs you £2 in petrol to get there and back because you're transporting a van for twenty-five miles. It's £2.75 for the stall, so that's £4.75. To make £10 you have to sell £20 if you're on a hundred per cent; if you're on less, which most people are, you would have to sell £25 or £30. I would say that you couldn't run a decent stall on under £1,500 worth of stock. You could do business if you hit lines; if you can buy one thing only and sell it then £150 can be done, but it's the clever buyer who does that.'

Gary D is a leather-worker and he and his partner have a stall in Petticoat Lane on Sundays and in Portobello Road on Saturday afternoons. He confirms the difficulty of getting a stall. 'They're all stallholders from way back; their fathers had the stalls. It's very difficult getting a place, you have to have your name down for years before the council will give you any indication.' The other alternative, as Gary D found out, is to be on the spot and take over a stall when the previous occupant leaves. Gary D's belts are sold mainly to tourists and, for him, it was quite an eye-opener. 'I was amazed,' he says, 'that tourists come all the year round, not just the summer. I sell almost as well in the winter.' On a good day he and his partner take about £180, half of which is profit. On a bad day it's much less. 'It's a living,' he says, 'but that's all.' Despite the rainy days, the shortage of space, the loading and reloading it can be a good way of selling and, as Sam S affirms, 'wherever you work it's peak trading day that day.'

Eight months later
'Yes, much as before,' says Sam S.

Part-time
Capital: started off with £50; turnover now in excess of £20,000
spends £15,000 a year on stock
3,000 square feet of storage space
two vans
casual labour about 50p an hour (children or O.A.P.s)
Income: C
Qualifications: none
(For more information about Gary D, see pages 108–11.)

CLOTHES SHOP

Barbara P's shop is full of flowing dresses, smocks, caftans, bags and wooden beads. Although she had only been open a month, very early days, the shop is the outcome of several years' work.

Stocking both her own designs and those of other suppliers, the shop developed out of Barbara P's work at home making custom-made clothes. Demand outgrew her flat, people were ringing up at all times of the day and night, so she decided to find a workshop, somewhere a bit more accessible and public. Instead she saw an advertisement in *Exchange & Mart* for a shop with flat above, an eighteen-year lease for £4,500.

She bought it. 'It was reasonably cheap,' says Barbara P, 'and although the lease isn't very long you will know whether it is going to work within about three years. I also wanted to live near where I worked, otherwise I just waste time going backwards and forwards.' Having decided to cross the watershed that lies between working freelance and running a business, Barbara P found that events just slotted into place. She already had a quarter of the capital and she borrowed the rest: 'The bank manager decided to take a chance on me.' The man who sold her the lease had started off in business fifteen years ago and was happy to help with advice. 'There are many people,' she says, 'who, if you ask and say, "What do you think is the best thing to do?" will actually tell you.'

Barbara P is cushioned against failure by her work as a teacher of textile design, macramé and weaving. She teaches adults fifteen hours a week which gives her enough income to bridge the inevitable gaps. 'It means that everything doesn't hinge on the shop and I have something regular,' she says. 'If you haven't got capital then this is essential.' She has spent very little on fixtures and fittings, partly because she hardly needed any and partly because 'you have to find out what is going to happen before you start spending lots and lots of money on doing the place up'.

Well, what is happening? 'Up to now I've been surviving on passing trade. Since it was just before Christmas it's been better than I hoped. In the New Year there will be a little piece in *Time Out* and a couple of other magazines are interested. Word of mouth is probably the best recommendation because in its way it is never-ending.' Barbara P is considering whether to advertise and 'risk having to stay up all night to keep up with it. I've had Yellow Pages trying to convince me that people sit around in the evening looking in the Yellow Pages for unusual dress shops. But you could over-advertise, get a condensed response which tapers out. The thing to aim for is something steady.'

Ever since she left art school Barbara P has made clothes for her friends and gradually she has developed her market; she now knows who she is catering for. 'I learnt how to cope with an order in the right way; it's very easy to be messy about the whole thing. You've got to be positive, offer a choice, take a deposit, give a time limit so people know exactly where they are.' Now that the shop has opened she is making clothes to stock the shop as well as to order. There is a twenty-five per cent markup on other people's work, which is sold sale or return. 'I want the things to be reasonably priced,' she says, 'although in a shop situation I price things more carefully than at home. This is where people part company, because they put the prices right up and get terribly exclusive. I think there's a good demand for well-made things in a middle price range.'

Nine months later
Barbara P's shop is flourishing in a small but steady way. Her customers, she finds, appreciate an uncomplicated and inexpensive made-to-order service although she now charges extra for fittings. 'If I didn't charge extra I would go out of business in six months,' she says. 'It's the difference between working now and again for friends and making a living.'

Part-time
Capital: £4,500 for lease of shop and flat
sewing machine cost £250

Income: A/B (from the shop)
Qualifications: textiles and fashion at Loughborough Art College for five years

GIFT SHOP

Up to Victorian times crocheted shawls, patchwork quilts and pot-pourris were the prerogative of the housewife. Then factory-made became the norm. In the swing back to hand-made goods small shops scattered throughout towns and villages play a decisive part.

Liza B and her two friends run such a shop. It started one evening. 'I was in a pottery class and next to me was the policeman's wife. I said to her, "Have you got anywhere to sell your things?" She said, "No," and I said, "What we need is a shop." I came out and saw an empty shop and we never looked back from that moment.'

Neither Liza B nor her partners had ever had any experience of running a shop. 'We couldn't add up so we got an accountant,' she says, 'and by then we knew we wanted a shop which was a service to people who made things, made a few of anything.' They rented the shop, the size of a living-room, for a low rent, put up shelving, painted the place, commissioned a shop sign, borrowed a counter and a till and raided their own houses for tables and chests of drawers. Each partner contributed £200; the shelving cost £140; the signs £50; paint and lighting another £50. Stock came from friends and local craftsmen and, with great trepidation, they opened in November 1973.

It has gone very well; nobody has made much money but nobody expected to. The shop is open three days a week and Saturday morning. About one hundred suppliers sell on a sale or return basis. Nobody is refused and the supplier must price his or her work; the shop adds fifty per cent markup on top of that. It is a just system. 'If it's badly made it doesn't sell and if it's too expensive it doesn't sell and after three months it goes back.' Nearly everything is eventually bought, though anything over £5 sells slowly. The shop is inundated with suppliers now that the word has spread and the difficulty is to strike the right balance. 'You've got to keep it varied,' says Liza B. 'What happens is that somebody brings in pincushions, they're seen in the shop and everybody thinks they can sell their pincushions here. We've been snowed under with Wombles this year because somebody demonstrated them on the tele. So I try and bring a new look to the shop; wherever I see something interesting I say, "Are you looking for new outlets?" I was at the Boat Show last night and I saw some painted stools and jugs and I left my card there.' At the moment Liza B is keeping an eye out for home-made cosmetics, musical instruments and goods for men ('we already have fishing flies and silk ties').

The shop is well out in the country, but it is on a busy road and attracts passing visitors, mainly Americans who buy light, flat things like scarves. A good half of the custom is local, within a radius of about eight miles; advertising they have found is a waste of time, customers come through the grapevine. Most buy presents and trade is seasonal, peaking at Christmas and Easter. At one point the partners considered encouraging coach loads, but thought better of it. 'A woman from Weston-super-Mare came in and said she had to close her shop, which was like ours, because the shoplifting was so terrific. If there's only one of you in the shop at a time your attention has only to be distracted for a minute.'

Although the shop is run in a light-hearted way, the partners sought professional advice and aim to be businesslike. They keep track of things: one stock book; one set of receipts in triplicate (supplier receives a copy, so does the book-keeper and the third stays in the shop). There is a daily sales book: one column for a description of the object sold, another for selling price, another for supplier's price and another for profit. The details for the daily sales book are recorded on labels: each object has a label attached to it which is removed when it is sold. The books have to be kept very neat and orderly and every two months suppliers are paid by cheque.

Although Liza B and partners do not make a living, could a shop like this be a viable commercial proposition? 'Yes,' she says, 'particularly if you lived over it and opened every day, and so long as you didn't want to make a fortune.' Since money isn't her motive, what is? 'You're putting people in contact with each other and the circle that evolves is really satisfying. It uses all your faculties: tidiness, aesthetic sense, patience, you've got to be good-tempered, you've got to remember your customers.'

Nine months later
'We closed the shop last Saturday and we've been stock-taking, clearing up and dealing with our 230 suppliers.' Why did you close? 'We weren't forced to close, but there were a number of reasons why we did: (1) because the premises were sold, (2) at the beginning of the year turnover was down and (3) one partner left and we couldn't get another. We had a sale in the last week and sold off a great deal of stuff.'

Part-time
Capital: £600
rent of shop £140 a year
Income: A
Qualifications: none

BUTCHER'S SHOP

Being a butcher is a dying (!) business. Paul C says so, and he has been in the trade for thirty years. With the price of meat rising, people are eating less of it both through choice and necessity. In one shopping parade he knows there are seven butchers and only enough trade for two; it is the overheads which are crippling. But if the trade is no longer what it was, Paul C and his partner, who is also his brother, are doing rather well with their seven shops. They are shrewd and hard-working and know all the ins and outs of the business through long experience. They might have succeeded in a number of occupations. They succeeded in this one through recognizing opportunities when they came and being in a position to take advantage of them, which is why they are included here.

Paul C learnt butchering in Ireland, first as an apprentice and then in Limerick manufacturing sausages. He went to night school in London, followed by a couple of years in a Canadian supermarket. Back in London he worked in a butcher's shop for eight or ten years, then got a job as a manager despite a warning from his previous employer that 'managers are born not made'. It didn't seem so. Then the lucky break came: about ten years ago the brothers began to rent their shops. They had £2,000 to £3,000, enough to start. The shops did well, they bought the freeholds and business has continued to be good. 'We didn't have a very good accountant at that time. He said, "Spend your money," but we didn't, we hung on to it, paid tax on it. We got a bit of good advice from a bank manager. He said, "If you're in business and you want to expand do it legitimately and pay tax on what you earn. After a couple of years you've got a fair deposit in the bank. If you fiddle tax you just can't borrow £4,000 or £5,000, there will be questions to answer from the Inland Revenue." '

Like most successful partnerships, this one runs on a combination of trust ('I don't look over his shoulder and he doesn't look over mine') and different responsibilities. They each run a shop, Paul C supervises the sausage factory at the back, his brother buys most of the meat. They have about thirty people working for them. 'It takes about five or six years to build up a team of this size, a good team who will look after the public well. They do their best, we don't expect too much of anybody. I think that's important, not to expect too much.' So how should the public be looked after? 'The secret is to be fair to the people you're dealing with,' he explains. 'If you bought a chicken and it was tough and you came to me I would say, "How much was it?" and you say, "£1.50," and I would say, "I'm dreadfully sorry, here is £1.50," that's the only way you can be. A lot of businesses these days people say, "You bought it, it's your hard luck." Or a housewife wants a bit of beef and before you cut it you say, "That's going to come to about £3.25." "Oh God," she says, "I only want to spend £1.50." So she tries something else, you haven't walked her into committing herself, to having made a mistake.'

Many shops depend on regular customers. 'We want to bring our customers back time after time after time,' says Paul C. 'You will be a good customer if I look after you; you may only spend £3 a week, but that's £150 a year. I want you back next week and the week after that because that's how I make my living, not just to give you some rubbish and never see you again. That's the main part of the business, to get a customer back again.' Paul C also sells his sausages to other butchers. 'Most work hard, but the fellow who doesn't try at all he goes to the betting shop or has a drink, leaves his business to somebody else to run. When everybody round you says, "Surrender," you have to have that little bit of gut in you which says, "Carry on." '

Eight months later
'We've opened one new shop and there's another one on the way, so we're not doing too badly.'

Full-time
Capital: £2,000 to £3,000 ten years ago (£1,000 buys enough meat per week for a busy shop)
electricity bill is £45 (to include the sausage factory)

small butcher will have overheads of £120 a week before wages
well-trained assistant's wages £60 to £70 in London, less in the country

Income: C

Qualifications: apprenticeship
night school
previous employment

ILLUSTRATION AGENCY

Not every agency is an illustration agency, very few are, but all agencies look both ways towards clients who provide work and clients who buy it. The agent enables A to meet B.

Jill M had tried a number of jobs including telephone sales and selling art kits to paraplegics; then she met Ken, her present partner, who was working in a tiny illustration agency. She started work with him and in a year they had quadrupled their billings. Jill M had found her *métier.* After two years they bought out the agency; that was three years ago and now they look after twenty-five illustrators covering a range of work from advertising through to book jackets and record sleeves.

What can they do for an illustrator? 'The way it happens,' says Jill M, 'is that the artist comes to the agent and says, "Look, this is my work; I would like you to keep me employed." Your job ideally is to keep them employed for the whole year. Of his total earnings we take twenty-five per cent which covers lunches, setting up the job, delivering, picking up, invoicing and collecting money.'

There is no contract between artist and agent, the artist can walk out anytime. The reason many choose an agent is because the agent can get work which they cannot; the agent is usually better equipped to handle contracts, royalties and so on; the agent saves them time; and the agent can give advice and suggestions about their work.

There is one other aspect which Jill M talks about: 'Someone once asked me, "If you left here what job would you walk into?" and I said "Probation Officer". We've had one attempted suicide, about six divorces, nervous breakdowns of wives, we've had abortions and running off to Egypt with a waiter. We've lost artwork in mid-flight because the plane blew up, we've lost it through Red Star and the post and we've had bounced cheques. They tend to use this place as a café, come in and you hear all their emotional problems.'

That is one half of the partnership. The other half, Ken, according to Jill M is 'the straight man. I think you have to have a Morecambe and Wise act in any partnership. He's the one who has four children, he's strictly the business one. I tend to be all fire and brimstone while Ken will just phone up and say, "I'd be grateful for the cheque." I'm the one who is pushing, getting ideas; Ken will sit down and say, "Let's work this out." I'm the kamikaze pilot and he takes my wings off occasionally. He's never done it so I've known about it.'

Jill M does not try to sell work. 'The only way you can do it is to say, "This guy is available, he will cost so much and he will have the job done in this amount of time." ' Nevertheless, a major part of her job is to ensure that her clients' work gets shown in as many places as possible. She says that it is a matter of commonsense. 'I go into supermarkets and find out who has what account by phoning up the advertising agencies and saying, "I've got some new artists, do you want to see?" I go into a record shop and see what record companies are using illustration. Or, if you see that a publisher is using illustrators like the ones you have, you ring up and say, "I admire your book jackets, Georgette Heyer or whatever, and I was wondering whether you would like to look at some more stuff," which they do.'

It is a rackety sort of business at times. 'I'm not very happy with my profession,' says Jill M. 'We have lots of bad agents; anybody can say they're an agent, they just need a telephone. But I want to be around until I'm sixty-five. When all the others are dead and buried they'll be saying, "I knew her when she was twenty-five or thirty-five and she was all right and she hasn't changed." That means more to me than any huge salary.'

Security isn't one of Jill M's anxieties. 'We live from day to day in this business,' she says. 'You have to go out and get in X number of thousands every month before you can even cover rates, telephone expenses, V.A.T. and expenses of a secretary. I like it. I would hate to come in nine to five and get my salary securely at the end of the month. I know that what I'm doing is largely because of my own initiative and talents. I'll never be sacked – though I could go bankrupt.'

Nine months later
'Since June,' says Jill M, 'I've been inundated with students leaving college and asking me to get them work. It's very disillusioning. I'm beginning to sound like my mother: "What they need is a bit of backbone, learn to stand on their own two feet." Most of them can't even draw. Nobody is concerned with old-fashioned things like draughtsmanship any more, the standard is really poor. But what can you do? The colleges don't teach them.'

Full-time
Capital: for usual office expenses and one assistant
Income: C
Qualifications: art school
previous employment

BOOK DISTRIBUTION

Tony B is out on the road every day. He distributes books – books which are produced by very small publishers, books which are too large, too odd, too alternative to be profitable to mainstream publishers. He fills a gap in publishing between producing a book and getting it to the bookshops, a gap which sometimes becomes a chasm as many authors well know. Books sometimes take weeks to arrive in a shop or they never arrive at all. None of this does the bookshop or the reader any good.

Tony B is not a large distributor; he is a one-man business, highly mobile, working from an eighteen hundredweight van which he tours all over the South, East Anglia and as far north as Liverpool and Manchester. As a book wholesaler he carries forty to fifty titles which he buys from publishers at fifty to sixty per cent discount and sells to bookshops at thirty to thirty-three per cent discount. He grosses £100 a week on average, £75 for expenses such as the hire of the van and petrol and £25 as a living wage. It is not very much for a hard week's work spent driving, visiting ten shops or so a day, showing books, lifting books; it is the driving and the talking which is exhausting day after day. 'It's fifty per cent flair, fifty per cent hard work,' he says. 'Each week I have to sell five hundred quid's worth of books to get my £100. If I carried more titles, say sixty, I could go a little slower, sell more books at each place.' With more books he would also need a larger van, and part of Tony's problem is under-capitalization. He was lent £2,000 by a friend but, since he buys books with cash and sells on credit, he never has any money to spare. 'I offer a cash discount within fifteen days which about half take advantage of,' he says. 'I usually replenish stocks about every four or five weeks, but of course all bookshops don't pay in four or five weeks.'

Four or five weeks is also the time between Tony B's visits to each bookshop. 'It doesn't always work but it's easiest to make it as regular as possible. I've just started a card index file with the names of all the shops, indexed under weeks, so I can see when a shop is due to be revisited.' Apart from the index file, Tony B keeps daily accounts of money coming in and money going out. He is also registered for V.A.T. and, since books are zero-rated, saves about £40 a month. Many self-employed people get in a tangle over accounts, how does he manage? 'I do my accounts every week,' he says, 'and transfer them into a ledger once a month. It takes about three hours a week and perhaps at the end of the year two days. I don't forget things because I write them down as I go along and put them together at the end of the week. Then, as far as I'm concerned, that information in there is correct and all I've got to do is transfer it into something presentable for tax purposes.'

Tony B learnt his accounts when he was working for Unicorn Books; when they moved to Wales, he started distributing. That was two years ago and he only left recently to start on his own. As a distributor, he had to visit all the shops, find his way around ('that's been one of the nicest things, getting to know this island') and keep a check on his stock. Part of his flair is getting on well with all types of booksellers and being able to talk informatively about books. 'I don't go in and say, "Buy this one, it's on television tonight," I just show people books and let them talk and ask questions. With established customers I can say, "This is a new one, you should take quite a few," or "I don't think you'll do very well with that." Eighty to ninety per cent of the time I know whether they're going to sell a lot or not.'

Bookshops still buy books, says Tony B, whatever the economic climate. He has sold books everywhere: England, Wales, Scotland, but 'although the deprived North is very pleased to scc people the distance between places is greater than in the South and you've eaten up most of the profit getting there.' Nevertheless, small-scale distribution can work well, especially with imported books, says Tony B. 'There are lots of American titles which sell extremely well over here, but only a few shops order them from the States. You need enough money to lay out for four or five months before it comes back.'

Eight months later
'I've started publishing my own books,' says Tony B, 'which is what I wanted to do all along. I've got five books (four are American underground) and two more on the way. I work on them in the evening. Another thing is the Arts Council grant for a van. That means I also distribute Arts Council funded publications. With this bigger van I shall be taking sixty to eighty titles. I'm still undercapitalized, but I might even give myself a wage increase after Christmas.'

Full-time
Capital: £2,000
van essential
no separate premises
Income: A
Qualifications: previous employment

CAR DEALING

As a second-hand car dealer Patrick G buys cheap and sells dear from his small showroom, which accommodates two cars and five more on the forecourt outside. He makes a good living buying from other dealers and either selling back to the trade or retail to private owners. 'As soon as I get a car,' he says, 'I clean it up, put it on the front, put price stickers on it and people see it as they go by. Or I advertise. Once you get established people ring you up.' The car leaves his hands with a three-month 'parts and labour' guarantee – good value, he feels. 'If you buy a car from a private person and it goes wrong you've got no comeback whatsoever, but if you buy one from a dealer you're protected under the Sale of Goods Act.' Buying and selling through the trade is a different matter; there you take the car as you find it. 'It's bread and butter,' he says, 'because I might not retail a car every week. If the retail side is quiet I can usually do a bit of trading.' There are three types of dealer, he says: (1) people working from home with old cars up to £200, (2) traders who buy from £200 to £1,000, (3a) dealers who have a showroom and retail and (3b) traders through and through with high turnover and low profit margins. Cars occasionally circulate for months if they are currently unpopular with the buying public.

Patrick G reckons the motor trade works in five-year cycles. 'We're just on the up now; car prices have doubled in just over a year which helps the second-hand car market tremendously. People cannot afford the change so they are looking for a late, low-mileage car, which is why I am specializing in that.'

There's an art to selling cars, so they say; it's more than being a good mechanic and more than knowing which cars are saleable and which are not – though that helps. It is also a question of building up contacts on the buying as well as the selling side. Patrick G learnt the trade over eighteen months as a salesman for Volvo agents. He had no previous selling experience and his mechanical knowledge was founded on tinkering around with old cars to supplement a student grant. Mechanical work, he says, is easy: 'If you can take something to pieces and put it together again you can work on a car, it's as simple as that. Diagnosing a fault can be a bit of a problem, but that's a problem for everyone. Most faults are fairly clear-cut; you might have to be a left-handed dwarf to get at it, but that's another story.' The job as a salesman 'gave me the basis I needed,' he says, 'and taught me how to sell. The main objective was to take new and used cars, take cars in part exchange and judge them for yourself. Two things can happen to a part exchange. You either retail it or sell it to a trader and someone else will retail it eventually. A Mercedes agent doesn't want to retail Volvos. We were selling Volvos so we would buy them.'

With contacts in the trade and £1,000 in hand he set up on his own, slowly at first, working as a paid mechanic and buying and selling the occasional car on commission. 'I spent last April to December checking that I was capable of making a living on my own,' he says. 'I was quite prepared to go back and get another job.' It wasn't necessary. Two months ago he bought and equipped a showroom for £2,000. A car dealer could start with £40, he admits, and 'buy an old banger and retail it for anything between £50 and £100 depending how sensibly he bought it. You've still got to live in that time so you're not increasing your capital.' Patrick G's nine-month gestation was spent 'looking around for more trade contacts where I could buy cars regularly, looking for more retail outlets where I had guaranteed sales rather than having to advertise all the time. When you're starting you don't want to tie all your money up in one car, you can't go to work. You want to have a car sold before you buy it.'

There are recognized places to advertise. *Exchange & Mart* is very good, says Patrick G, for cars up to £1,000. Expensive cars are advertised in *Motor*, *Autocar* and the evening papers. Local papers, he has noticed, encourage people who like looking at cars but have no intention of buying one. Dealers sometimes run into problems with the public in other ways. Not everybody wants a string of cars in various stages of repair along their road ('which is why I got a showroom'). Patrick G once solved that problem by offering to service his neighbours' cars at a discount. It had a wonderful effect. Council regulations are strict about such things as mechanical work, re-spraying and even price stickers. Bookwork is another hazard; everything is done in triplicate and V.A.T. is hungry for any amount of information. At bottom, the real salesmanship, he says, 'is being able to relate to people at their own level. I might have an immaculate car, but someone might not buy it because he didn't like the look of me. When you start off you have to sell the kind of car you look like.'

Seven months later
'When the car sales are going O.K. that's fine,' says Patrick G, 'but the rest of the time I sit around twiddling my thumbs. So I'm starting a car hire business, with a couple of cars, to balance things up a bit. The showroom used to be a car hire firm and we get lots of enquiries. I've got a partner now and we shall do it between us. We are also starting a car tuning service, giving a full diagnosis of the engine and getting it to perform properly.'

Full-time
Capital: £1,000
showroom later cost £2,000 for eighteen-month lease (recently renewed for twenty years)
Income: C
Qualifications: employment as car salesman

ANTIQUES

i. Book dealing

Scene: basement of Kenilworth Hotel in London. Event: meeting of Provincial Booksellers' Fairs Association. Action: book meets bookseller. It is an antiquarian and second-hand book mart, dealers buying from other dealers, the public buying, everybody stocking up and exchanging news until the next fair. Michael H was there. He has been a fanatic bookman, he says, since his first job selling newspapers on a Smith's stand. He progressed to working freelance as a publisher's rep, which he did for fourteen years, and slowly the antiquarian side evolved until he now buys and sells books on English local history and fishing. 'I spend half my life travelling around the country,' he says. 'We organize twenty-four book fairs a year and this is a substantial part of the business these days. Apart from book fairs I've been in Somerset, Wiltshire, Stratford, most of southern England in the last month.'

Michael H makes his living from knowing that a book

priced at £3 can be sold for £6. It is buying in a general market and selling in a specialized one. That kind of knowledge doesn't come easily. It is composed of part experience, part indefinable flair and part hard work building up a market. Michael H buys ten per cent of his books from auctions, but the bulk of his stock comes from other booksellers. He sells about a quarter of his books at fairs this way: 'Gerald usually brings me up a box of books on my subject and I bring aviation books for Alan. The rest is sold by catalogue.' A dealer's catalogue is his market, a carefully cultivated and prized possession. Michael H prints a catalogue about six times a year and it gets sent to collectors all over the country and abroad. He adds to his list by advertising in fishing journals.

Michael A, however, has no mailing list and he hardly ever goes to auctions or buys from the trade. He runs one of the few second-hand bookshops in south London. 'People can bring the contents of their attics to a shop,' he says, 'whereas they wouldn't go to a private address. About half my books are sold in the shop, the rest at fairs like this one.' Most of the books sold are nineteenth century; earlier books are rare and expensive. Some books always sell better than others: those with fine bindings or illustrations sell, theology does not sell (been written about too often), fiction does not sell unless it is of intrinsic value. Books which always sell, says Michael A, are those about old customs or country life or something discovered like 'the sex life of the crab', or 'diseases of craftsmen'. Michael A details the progress of an antiquarian book: 'It starts with people producing them from dustbins, bric-à-brac shops and second-hand shops. They gradually move into the hands of the specialist. They may go into auctions and be bought by dealers here or abroad, they may come to fairs. They move on. They may go into the hands of dealers again or into universities or institutions where they are used as reference books. If they go to a collector and he dies, while his body is still warm his wife sells the books and they come into the open market again.'

One practice which is spoken of as if it is a secret vice is that of breaking up books to get at the prints. 'The illustrations are sometimes cut out,' says Michael A, 'then colour washed and framed to make prints. It is deplorable for a good book, but it does pay the rent. This is a trade which is connected with investment and the prints as fine art may themselves be an investment.'

Stephen C used to be an acquisitive collector; now he not only collects, but also buys and sells modern first editions of creative writing and books on bygone aspects of English life such as canals, windmills and folk lore. He also has a shop – 'with all its overheads it's an expensive luxury.' Postage is another large expense. 'We send one thousand catalogues and each catalogue is 12½p second class postage. You have your American library buyer and, say, he gets six catalogues that morning and five of them are seamail, six weeks old. I bet they go straight into the bin. If you send that catalogue airmail it will cost 50p and he still might not order.'

Stephen C's customers are mainly private collectors. 'The golden age of the American institutional budgets are dead and gone,' he says, 'but I'm finding that private people are buying books however little money they have. There's something about a first edition; you must have it, particularly if you are forming an author collection.' He pulls down one book after another. 'This is John Fowles's first book; this is the first book that Rex Whistler illustrated. One of the great things in modern first editions is literary associations: *The Forest Giant* by Adrien Le Corbeau published by Jonathan Cape in 1924 and translated by J.H. Ross, which is a pseudonym for Lawrence of Arabia, one of his four pseudonyms. You wouldn't know that, a lot of booksellers wouldn't know that, would price it five bob. You see it's £12.'

Ten months later

Despite an earlier attempt to open a bookshop, which then never paid off, Michael H has tried again. This time 'it's an art gallery and second-hand and antiquarian bookshop combined,' he says. 'We sell English topographical books and nineteenth-century topographical watercolours. I have a manageress and it's been going about two months, rather well in fact, we can afford to eat nearly every day now.'

'The book fairs are doing very well,' says Michael A. 'We now have a provincial one every month. I think they are getting more popular as bookshops tend to die out. I've still got the shop of course. With the aid of alcohol and a reliable staff we're carrying on.'

'It's a difficult financial period,' says Stephen C, 'but people are still buying books. We've just sent out a catalogue and half of the books listed in it have been sold in the first week.'

MICHAEL H
Full-time
Capital: anything, he says, between £100 and £20,000 car essential
Income: C
Qualifications: previous employment

ii. Islamic antiques

The art and antiques market is in a constant state of flux, everything on the move, changing hands, shifting from one part of the globe to another. It is a market like any other; although its goods are local in origin, they are international in buying power.

Peter V is one pair of changing hands. He buys Islamic antiques and rugs in Turkey, Greece, Syria and Egypt and sells them to dealers and collectors all over the world. It all started when he was a student five years ago and began buying nineteenth-century kilims in Greece and the Middle East. At that time very few people knew anything about these nomadic prayer rugs; nowadays they hang in every Bond Street in the world. Peter V discovered that he had an eye for what was good and valuable: 'If you walk into a room with a few china dolls, a few pots and pans and amongst them you have an Islamic bronze you don't notice it, it's hardly recognizable. But if I approach a collector of Islamic art and say, "I've got a thirteenth-century Mosul bronze," and tell him that there is a similar one in such and such museum, it compares with that, it is the work of such and such craftsman, it seems to be from there, with all the expertise behind it, then it is a totally different object from what he would have seen for himself, not even trusted his taste in the little old lady's room or in a smart crooked dealer's shop in Cairo, where he doesn't really know if it is a real one or a dummy one.'

Although he belongs mentally and spiritually to the Middle East, Peter V says he has very few qualms about exporting antiques to the West. They don't treat them properly at home. He quickly points out that 'in most countries there is a law which ostensibly protects the national heritage and forbids taking out anything which is earlier than the twentieth century. But you go to their museums and there are damp basements full of the most incredible carpets rotting away. I saw a very early carpet, one of the best types of carpet in the world. It was rolled and then the roll was folded in four. It is a criminal thing to do to a carpet because it breaks it; when I unrolled it, it was in four pieces.' The definition of 'national heritage' is a very thorny one at the best of times. If Britain kept only those works of art made here the galleries would be empty. All the same, isn't it difficult to take antiques out of a country? 'More through ignorance than illegality,' he says. 'I came out of a Moslem country with fifteen very good rugs. One of them, the only one with nasty chemical colours, I was forced to buy by the dealer because he wanted a price for the lot. This rubbishy one had a star of David. When the customs opened them they cleared the lot and when they saw the last one they freaked out.'

Peter V first started buying and selling to pay for his studies; then as his knowledge of antiques, and of Islamic design in particular, developed dealers and collectors began contacting him. 'You don't need to advertise,' he says. 'Other people will find out what you have. It's very mysterious but that's how it is. It is superfluous to have a shop, the things sell anyway.' In fact he tries to sell as little as possible. He and his partner have taken a long-term view of the market for Islamic antiques and have decided that it has a long way to go. The day that Arabs start seeing their own antiques in museums will be the day that they stop cutting up carpets – or selling them to the West. With a combination of sound business sense and cultural philanthropy Peter V hopes to re-sell to the Middle East. 'These things should go back to their origins,' he says, 'where those who made them can see them and take pride in their own creations. I get terribly upset when I see French furniture or fake plastic flowers in Arab houses. Now they are acquiring financial muscle I would like to see a renaissance.'

Nine months later
'The same thing never arises twice,' says Peter V, 'and there is really no definite pattern. If there was, I probably wouldn't be working in this field.'

Part-time
Capital: 'You can never say, any two situations are quite different.'
no separate premises but storage space
Income: B
Qualifications: none

IMPORTING AGENT

In a highly competitive market the one who is quickest off the mark at least gets a sprinting start over his competitors. He has also to offer the right goods as Antonio B, an agent and importer of onyx and alabaster lamps from Spain to England, has found out. 'The real skill in selling', he says, 'is finding out what the client wants and transmitting this to the Spanish manufacturer. Many people come over here with goods, just on the off-chance, and I can see that they are not going to sell.' The first thing, then, is to find out what people want and it can be done 'if the client trusts you. If he trusts you, you will have access to all sorts of information.' The technical business of importing or exporting is comparatively straightforward after that.

Antonio B has lived in this country for eight years. For the first six years he worked for a translation agency and as an interpreter for Spanish businessmen coming over here. He once interpreted for a manufacturer of onyx lamps. 'He had come over here without any knowledge of the market and we started from scratch, looking at directories, trying to find manufacturers of lamps and making appointments.' After ten days Antonio B was offered the job of representative and without any previous experience he agreed to sell lamps on commission. When the lamps arrived from Spain, however, there were a couple of bad sales and to avoid returning the goods Antonio B bought and stored four hundred lamps in his flat. He had to sell them, but there were a lot of identical lamps on the market. 'I decided to change the shapes of the lamps,' he says, 'and I started importing different fittings. I experimented on shapes just to find out tastes, what people liked. In the end I sold them all just by finding the right shape.' But tastes change. Antonio B had a lot of brown onyx lamps 'which was a colour nobody wanted to know about because everybody had the idea that onyx ought to be green. It was only because I was stuck with stocks that I had to persevere with the brown onyx. Now, after two years, brown is a top colour. There are other factors, of course; green is sometimes difficult to get and more expensive.'

Meanwhile, manufacturers who were buying onyx were also buying alabaster, not just lamps but ashtrays, boxes, eggs, jars and figures. Antonio B found a supplier of alabaster and broadened his range. He added small wooden carts to his list and these carts showed how vulnerable the gift market is to undercutting. 'For two years there was an incredible sale of these carts,' he says, 'and since then it has been copied in plastic and the prices have immediately dropped.' Other items, particularly if they can't be imitated, may have a steadier sale, for example 'brown onyx which doesn't seem to come from many other places. In alabaster prices are lower than the competitor, which is Italy. In Spain we don't have the knowhow of finishing or colouring alabaster but in white there is no problem.' With new products Antonio B imports a small quantity – about £1,000 worth – to assess the market with an immediate supply of samples and stocks. After two years he has discovered what will sell and what will not. Spanish firms will give him three or four months' credit, simply because they trust him; it is easier, he reckons, to get £10,000 credit from a Spanish manufacturer than £500 from a British bank.

As an agent Antonio B's commission ranges from five to ten per cent. Not only does he have to find buyers, but he also has to see that 'the buyer and seller are on good terms. If the buyer says, "I haven't got the right quantity," or "This is bad quality," or "We have so many breakages," I have to keep the peace.' Ideally, Antonio B would like to leave the importing side and concentrate on selling, on 'becoming a buying agent for half a dozen importers because the real importers buy in large quantities providing the prices are right. It allows you to travel and find manufacturers who are willing and able to sell over here and to try and connect the two things together. The task is to persuade the Spanish manufacturer to produce what England would like to consume.'

Four months later

'I am gradually becoming a direct importer of goods,' says Antonio B. 'This is partly because it is very difficult to return merchandise once it has been imported and sometimes the previous importer won't accept it because of economic difficulties or disputes over quality. So I sell it here. The other reason is that I get very good credit from Spanish manufacturers. There are now three of us. Two of us are partners and the third is a sales agent.'

Full-time
Capital: for typewriter and usual office expenses
office rent £60 a month
warehouse space (large enough for two large container loads) £40 a month including handling charges (handling and storage charges are two per cent of the price of goods)
car essential
Income: B
Qualifications: none (in this case fluent Spanish is very useful)

Chapter Four
House & Home

HOME DESIGN

Not many people see three years' work go up in three-quarters of an hour, but it happened to Paul O. He was also deprived of a home when the house he was working on – re-plumbing, re-wiring and re-furbishing – caught fire in 1970. With no financial resources, he decided to make a temporary living by hiring himself out as a 'repairer, re-arranger and maker of bits and pieces'. He has been doing this ever since. All his work is one-off designs, whether for the furnishings and fittings of a kitchen or a scheme for a foldaway bed. People come to him with their problems, very often problems of space. A typical problem can go like this: two people live in a one-room flat with alley kitchen and tiny bathroom. They have vast quantities of books, records and three cats. At the moment it looks like a scruffy bedsit with planks thrown against the wall and curtains pulled across the bed. How can it be turned into an attractive flat with twice as much space to play in? Solution: design and make furniture which folds, tucks and disappears into the wall when it is not needed.

After time spent as an engineering and industrial design student and researcher into laboratory equipment, Paul O decided to become a practical man and volunteered to improve his parents' house, stage by stage, learning as he went, if they would agree to pay him a minimum wage. To their credit they accepted. 'I did that for seven years,' he says, 'not all the time, but gradually I built up a full working knowledge of carpentry and all the rest of it and I was responsible for everything in the house, all the fittings and furnishings.' It was, as he says, 'extremely tentative at the beginning, I had very few tools. I didn't have a plane and I borrowed a saw. Now I have a couple of hundred quid's worth of tools, though nothing very glamorous.' He bought, cheaply, some shop counters for sinks and storage units. 'It's a good way for anybody to start, by converting existing pieces of furniture,' he says, 'because you are relieved of the problems of designing from the bottom up for structural strength and for getting everything square.'

While serving his apprenticeship, as it were, Paul O improved the house he was living in and then came the fire. He has never been out of work since; he makes enough money to live on but not enough 'to buy myself out of favours. If I had a bit of capital I would buy a workshop instead of having to saw wood in the garden.' His pricing is partly at fault, he admits. 'I get interested in jobs and I get what we call ideas and they work out but take three times as long. At the end you realize you were four weeks instead of two, that it cost not a couple of quid chasing after this and that but seven or eight and you're really fagged out. The job is done, the person is happy and they've willingly accepted a ten to twenty per cent increase because they know it's good value. But they won't accept a hundred per cent increase.' Part of the answer is to simplify the design so that 'you have a modular way of making things instead of completely comprehensive all-over speculation every time you take on a new piece of work'.

When he first meets a prospective customer, Paul O discusses the work and 'asks them what they're prepared to spend, what they've seen in the shops and what seems worthwhile expenditure'. Details and basic scale drawings go in a folder and the materials are bought or picked up from previous work. At that stage he takes fifty per cent in advance from the customer. Only once has somebody not paid him. Apart from individual customers, Paul O has worked as a sub-contractor for an architect and vows never to do it again. 'It looked profitable when it was offered several years ago,' he says, 'but so many things did not run according to plan. I would turn up to find that the place didn't have any floors and I would have to find a useful way of killing time and there is no useful way. This is where I score when I'm working on my own, because I do the plumbing and wiring and everything.'

Nine months later
For the last four months Paul O has been working on a £2,000 kitchen and, in the process, discovered a new way of pricing his work. Instead of basing his price on time and materials (i.e., what it costs him), he estimated on the price of an equivalent ready-made kitchen (i.e., what it would otherwise cost his customer to buy). This method benefits him financially and is considered just all round.

Full-time
Capital: none
tools worth about £200
back garden for sawing and hammering
van essential
Income: B
Qualifications: none

DECORATING

Many actors find themselves out of work at one time or another and David K was no exception. As a student he worked as a decorator for his father, simply because 'I needed to support myself with a certain amount of freedom and without the restrictions of being in a normal job.' He has worked in this way for the last ten years, finding clients through personal recommendation and picking up experience and new techniques as he went along. 'I started off doing painting and decorating,' he says, 'and then it extended to paper-hanging. I even specialize in that; hanging a lot of the modern wallpapers, the vinyl and foil ones, fabrics and silks.' Another speciality is intricate painting and working with gold leaf; one job was sub-contracting to paint cornices in Buckingham Palace. 'Lots of people try their hand at decorating,' he says. 'Materials are simpler and everything becomes easy and few people specialize. So if you do specialize invariably you will corner that end of the market.'

David K charges £12 a day for his labour ('I can remember when it was £5; every six months I review it again'), plus the cost of materials and expenses. One job does not always follow straight on from another and he admits that he would be better off if he worked for an employer, but 'I have an aversion to it in every way. The nearest I've come to it is in sub-contracting, when the standard of work is taken out of your hands, what you do and the way in which it is done. If you're lucky enough to work for somebody who does demand good standards and is well organized, it's fine, but usually it isn't like that, you waste a lot of your time whereas it's only natural to get on with it and do it.'

One of the most important parts of the job, he says, is finding out exactly what people want – and that isn't always easy. 'Invariably you will be given a magazine and told, "I want that," but if you have a little semi-detached you can't turn it into an Italian villa. Often it is a matter of people wanting to superimpose something that is totally unrealistic and not seeing the potential of what they really have.' A house is also a home, dear to the owner's heart, and many hearts want it to be the same as it always has been, regardless. In the end 'you can't impose your taste,' says David K, 'you have to remember that you're really the servant of the people you're working for.' For all that, his personal taste is often called upon. Experience in stage design helps: 'I used to work in austere companies so you had to create the maximum effect with the minimum amount. You realize how easily, by introducing one colour or item, you can completely create an atmosphere, often very simply.'

Working on his own David K maintains the minimum of equipment and outlay – just a car with a roof-rack. He has thought of expanding, 'employing people, with a yard and all the rest of it, but then you lose contact, you're an administrator and rely on other people's skills. And the bigger you are the harder you fall. When you're a one-man band you haven't got much to lose – but you don't stand much chance of growth either.'

At the moment he is just about to grow. In a new project getting off the ground David K will be working alongside another interior designer. He will be employed for a few days at a time, lending his practical experience to complement the other's technical and drawing abilities. 'It's a natural development,' he says. 'At times I get browned off continually painting people's bedrooms and I would like to do something with more scope.' Two designers, he reckons, can cover far more ground working together than working separately. 'You can only be in one place at any one time,' he says, 'either travelling round jobs in progress or researching them or at the drawing board. If there is just one person he has to be on site a lot of the time which keeps him right away from his drawing board. With two of you a much greater volume of work can be maintained.'

Nine months later

'The design project didn't materialize,' says David K, 'because there wasn't enough work to keep the two of us going. After I picked up the threads again I had lots of offers for decorating work. What I'm finding now is that do-it-yourself is fading out a bit; people have tried their own decorating and the results aren't good enough. My prices have also gone up to £13 or £14 a day and nobody seems to mind that. I think they accept that costs and materials are always going up.'

Full-time
Capital: none
tools (including ladder) worth about £200
van or car essential, with roof-rack
Income: now C
Qualifications: none

PLUMBING

'I used to help my father in the holidays and he said to me, "What are you going to do when you leave school?" Of course I didn't have a clue. He said, "If you want to work in the building industry, I should take a trade; of all the ones you have seen which one would you prefer?" ' Bernard D set out to become a plumber. He worked, firstly, for his father and then as an 'improver' for another firm while he took City and Guilds examinations in plumbing, heating and ventilation.

After about seven years he thought, 'I know enough to be getting on with,' and re-joined his father, doing small jobs like sink units, wash basins and bathrooms. When his father retired he became self-employed with lots of misgivings. Doubts were unfounded. Finding work is no problem; he is booked up two or three months in advance, one job leading to another, all within a five-mile radius. Paperwork is a major bugbear, that and organizing a working life where he may do many jobs in one week and never know in advance how long each one is going to take. 'I've got a diary which is really phone messages,' he says, 'but I never put down "Mr Smith is going to take four days." I used to do that and it never worked out. So now I put, "Wednesday I've got to go out and I think it will take a day." So I book Wednesday and it might take me to Thursday but I'll still be busy Thursday whether this job overlaps or not. So I don't commit myself every day. I'll commit myself to two, maybe three, jobs a week.' The rest of the time is spent on emergency work: the 'water is dripping through the ceiling' variety and other quick jobs, such as . . . 'A woman rang up tonight; her radiators aren't working. She's an old customer so I should help her. It could take half a day, it might take an hour.' In these circumstances forward planning is difficult. 'I should write down, "Mr Smith is thinking about a shower in six weeks," and then look up two weeks in advance to see what my work commitments are.'

Most of Bernard D's customers, about eighty per cent, come to him through other customers. He also keeps his name in the Yellow Pages – his only advertising. 'Unless you want to expand a lot you really shouldn't have to advertise,' he says. Most people ring in the evening or at any rate after half past three in the afternoon, when his wife gets in. The pair of them are sometimes jumping up and down all evening answering the phone. He accepts jobs up to about £500 work, estimating for the larger ones and charging by the hour for the smaller ones. It works out about £3 an hour.

Apart from the business side, plumbing suits Bernard D very well, 'though it can get a bit boring if you're in an empty house; you end up talking to yourself. But I don't have to clock in; I can start at seven and end at three o'clock without asking anybody.' The main thing about being a good plumber, he says, 'is that you do a reasonable job for a reasonable price. The price is not as important as the work you do.' What about those maverick plumbers who charge you £10 if they so much as replace a tap washer? 'Three-quarters of the stories I've heard,' he says, 'it's been the emergency service that's at fault. It really depends who is driving the van that day whether you get a proper plumber at work.' He tells a horrific story: somebody 'called in an emergency plumber because her cold water wasn't running very well. He said he would have to connect it to the mains because bigger pressure would push the blockage out. He connected the mains to the hot-water tank which burst and brought the ceiling down. Then he told her it was going to break anyway. It cost about £170 and all it probably needed was a bit of wire poking down the pipe; the plumber didn't know what he was doing.' So what is the best way of learning what to do? 'I found I learned far more working for a plumber than I did at school,' he says. 'Unless you're planning big projects you don't need to know half the calculations I was taught. The do-it-yourself magazines are quite helpful on the theory side but you can't beat practical work.'

Seven months later
Still plumbing.

Full-time
Capital: basic tools cost about £100
car or van essential
no separate premises
Income: C
Qualifications: City and Guilds examinations
previous employment

BUILDING

Building had a notorious reputation as a business of get-rich-quick entrepreneurs who disappeared overnight leaving a trail of half-finished houses behind them. Throughout the upheavals of the building boom and into the stringent seventies the small local builder was a perennial amongst the fast-fading annuals. Derek E belongs to this breed, although he has only been working as a builder for the last eighteen months. He had always been a do-it-yourself man and learnt the basics of building by hiring the village builder to renovate his own house and working as his labourer. Then, as a farmer, he did his own building, but it wasn't until he went to Yorkshire that he joined up with two others and started taking on outside jobs. 'The difficult thing is making a start,' he says. 'We found postcards in newsagents' windows the best thing, but then you do a couple of jobs and the news spreads very quickly by word of mouth.'

They found a market in renovating cheap, dilapidated property, 'mainly bought by young people. It needed an inside loo and bathroom, walls knocked down, that sort of thing.' With a van and roof-rack and about £200 worth of tools accumulated over the years, Derek E is equipped to tackle brick-laying, concreting, plastering, decorating and plumbing. 'The ideal', he says, 'is to have two or three blokes – one, say, a joiner, one a plumber and another an electrician. In any case there are quite a lot of jobs difficult to do single-handed.' Now that he has moved to a community in Suffolk, Derek E is working with a joiner there. 'You try and diversify your skills as much as you can,' he says. 'I've taught Chris to plaster, which he had never done and never thought he could do. Plastering is a thing which has a fair amount of mystique attached to it. Again, I would like to know more about electronics.' Their first big job is on a house in a low-cost housing area in Ipswich. It will need a new roof and their boards will hang on the scaffolding for anybody to see and to approach with new work.

Another way of finding work is to link with an architect, as Derek E did in Yorkshire: 'He got in with the local Pakistani population and when they said could he recommend a builder he would suggest us' – a useful link-up. Apart from familiarity with planning laws a builder needs to know the building regulations 'which vary in parts of the country. I've only just discovered,' he says, 'that in the next district you can't any longer use brass fittings, they've got to be gunmetal because of the composition of the water.'

Financially, Derek E lives quite simply and has few administrative overheads. If the two of them took on a £1,000 job it might take a month or six weeks, for which they earn about £12 a day each. The cost of the materials is a heavy outlay, although 'you can arrange with the customer to make progress payments which at least cover the cost of your materials.' Estimating, he says, is the most skilful part of the job. 'If you quoted to do a job on the basis that it would take a month and you hit snags and it takes you two months your earnings are going to be half of what you expected. It's always a relief when you finish on time.'

Building work can be highly competitive. 'There is a big temptation to cut things too fine,' says Derek E. 'If you're employing a couple of chaps you've got to meet their wage bill every week, so you're desperate to keep them busy. If there are two or three of you working together and you're not earning anything you're prepared not to draw anything out. I think you ought to warn people not to embark alone on this sort of thing until they've had a fair bit of experience, because you can leave yourself wide open to all sorts of mistakes.'

Seven months later
'There are four of us now,' says Derek E. 'We've been joined by two learners and work is going pretty well. We had a slack period at the end of the summer, but now we're booked up six months ahead. It's all work with private houses, locally: extensions, roofing, brick-laying, that sort of thing. As people get to know about us we get more work, some of it in the village.'

Full-time
Capital: £200 worth of tools
van essential, with roof-rack
no separate premises
Income: B
Qualifications: none

FURNITURE RENOVATION

Sue M has a husband, three children, another on the way and a back room stuffed full of furniture in the process of being stripped. She enjoys working with wood; one of her previous activities was picture framing, but even more satisfying is taking in a 'tatty old chest of drawers covered with layers of paint and bringing it up a lovely mellow colour'. She and her husband, Bruce, began stripping furniture as a hobby. About a year ago, she bought a couple of kitchen chairs from a junk yard and, when they were sanded and polished, Bruce asked, 'Why don't you sell them?' Sue M picked up a chest of drawers off a rag and bone man in the street and rather laboriously stripped it; then, saving up her family allowance until she had £30, she bought a chest of drawers, three or four chairs and two tables.

'It was the beginning of the summer,' she says, 'and I worked outside. I put an advert in the local paper. The first person who came bought two chairs and wanted two more as well as a dining-room table. She paid me for the chairs which gave me the money for the table.' A local upholsterer also came and invited Sue M to sell her furniture in a monthly Saturday market, to be organized on the forecourt of his shop. 'That was the greatest impetus of all,' she says. 'I never worked so hard in my life. On the day, we loaded up the furniture at nine o'clock and somebody was already waiting for us. I sold everything that day plus the things half finished and ordered.' The upholsterers also had a good day, and Sue M now works mostly towards the next month's sale.

The furniture which Sue M likes is basic English, often pine or walnut, the chairs of beech with elm seats. The biggest demand, she finds, is for chests of drawers and seamen's chests. 'What is so appealing about it,' she says, 'is that it is so plain and simple you couldn't improve on it in any way. Most of it is a good deal better than the modern furniture.' Bruce M explains further. 'I think there's a reaction against plastic stuff so more people want better quality furniture such as we like and provide.'

At the beginning, Sue M used to 'go out in the car, take

the kids and look for stuff – but it's very time-consuming'. Now she buys from an antique dealer who does house clearance and has introduced her to other dealers and shops. All her supplies of furniture come this way. Over a period of time she has learnt to judge the quality of the wood lying underneath the paint, what will reward stripping and what is best forgotten. Back home, the furniture is taken outside to a convenient concrete yard, stripped, hosed down and left to dry. Occasionally, pieces get sent off for professional stripping, but 'there are so many people', she says, 'who plonk the stuff in, turn up the thermostat, leave it for a couple of days and it is ruined.'

Sanding and polishing follow on. Sometimes an otherwise good piece of furniture needs repairing and Bruce and Sue M carry out small repairs. Handles and other fittings are often missing or need replacing and Sue M scours local shops to find the right sort of fittings. Files are stacked on her shelves: records of where to get supplies, records of 'shops and what they're selling and how much their prices are. This is an invaluable compendium,' she says. Selling prices are fairly uniform. 'A chest of drawers will always cost £25; if you buy one with unusual handles it will be £28 and so on; but you never get anything less than £25.'

Nine months later

Sue M was in hospital for seven weeks before the baby was born. During that time her eldest son managed the Saturday market, her husband bought some furniture and dealers kept back things for her. Now, four months later, she is carrying on as before with some useful publicity from the local newspaper. 'Before I had the baby,' she says, 'I was determined to keep going. My only worry was that I might not be able to, but I find that I can. I'm also thinking of having a shop, perhaps one at the end of the road, or of going in with someone else to sell my stuff.'

Part-time
Capital: £30 for first stock
storage space and yard
car or van essential
family assistance
Income: A
Qualifications: none

STEREO REPAIR

Olaf U is living in a community of thirty adults and fifteen children with his wife and small son. He repairs stereo equipment which he collects from an electrical shop and brings back to a tiny 'laboratory' bristling with knobs, cables and apparatus. Then, restored to health, he returns them to the shop. He charges £2 an hour, which is enough to support himself and his family. Ever since he was a child, Olaf U has been interested in electrical equipment – especially stereos – the way some people always fiddle around with cars. After university and working on Saturdays in a workshop, he set up on his own. He spread the word round amongst his friends and advertised in *Time Out*, but now most of his work comes through the shop and he can take it away and 'give it a full test and check it over properly'. The other alternative is to 'go round with a screwdriver and a little volt meter and say, "We'll fix that up in no time," which doesn't encourage the customer to feel at all confident.' Not an approach he would recommend.

After eight or nine years Olaf U says he knows less than when he started; this can't be true, but it is a reminder of how quickly new products come on to the market and 'it's helpful to read magazines and do your own *Which?* research,' he says. 'In any case people ask you, so you need to know.' For somebody starting up, basic equipment costs about £100 and is sufficient for most stereos. Olaf U points out that no two problems are quite the same: 'You may find that you can't do the first one, or the second, and by the third you wonder, "Am I any good at all?" ' Persistence pays off. If it doesn't, the recalcitrant machine can always be handed over to another, more experienced person with little lost except a touch of pride. Once skills are established they become easier to sell. 'If I was starting again,' says Olaf U, 'I would do it with one other person who is commercially presentable and who would go to shops and say, "We'll take all your repair work, we'll charge you and you can charge your customers whatever you like; we'll guarantee the work and we'll do it inside a week," and we'll take all your troubles from you in effect. That is how I would do it. The chap who is best at talking is not necessarily the best at fixing the amp.'

While at first one may have to take anything offered, choosing the type of work preferred is surely the cherry on top of the self-employed cake. Olaf U suffers, he says, from a personal inability to say 'no'. 'I've spent a lot of time', he says, 'in running around after small jobs which don't pay very well. Inexpensive equipment is sometimes hardly worth repairing, whereas somebody with hundreds of pounds worth will pay to get it working properly.' People get very fussy about their stereos and his work has led Olaf U into swampy regions, as he explains: 'When people get quite neurotic about their stereos it's not just a hi-fi – it's their little baby with its problems. They buy something else and it's not quite what they want so they buy something else. It's not rational at all. There are a few people who sit and listen to the music, and for those it is fun to work, but the others are cases of "I think my volume control knob is wobbly; I'll have a new amp because of it," and that's not fun anymore.'

Olaf U is looking for other areas of work. He and others in the community, including Derek E (see page 79), are investigating solar roof heating which is already commercially viable and looks set for the future. One other project, along the same lines, is the erection of windmills for generating electricity. They have already put up a windmill for a self-sufficient doctor living in a windy place in Norfolk. The windmills are sold in kit form by Conservation Tools and Technology, but even so 'it's a bit complicated,' says Olaf U. 'There were two control panels and you have to fit together unusual bits and pieces, find the right sort of cables.' The kits are quite expensive, though eventually they pay for themselves. It is still early days, but as far as Olaf U is concerned it is a long-term project.

Seven months later
'We are getting more work installing windmills,' says Olaf U. 'I have had a preliminary site inspection and customers' estimates for four or more windmills including one local one. I also make useful little gadgets which are not in the C.T.T. kit. We have also installed solar panels for a private swimming pool in Hendon, though it was a long way to go and we hardly made any money from it.'

Part-time
Capital: £100 for basic equipment (Olaf U's stereo repair equipment is worth about £2,000)
essentials are volt meter £10, oscilloscope £25 and signals generator (home-made)
car useful for collecting stereo equipment
no separate premises but small laboratory area
Income: A
Qualifications: electronics degree
previous part-time employment

LETTING ROOMS

Many people with a spare room or two would like to let it off and earn themselves some money into the bargain. It would be so easy, they muse, to put in a gas ring and turn the guest room into a bedsit and how nice it would be. Others, fingers burnt, swear never again or talk extensively about unpaid phone bills or yards of damp washing hanging in the bathroom. Everybody has a different recipe for successful landlord/tenant relations, but whatever is chosen must fit individual circumstances; there is no single well-tried formula.

First of all tenants, under law, enjoy a good deal of protection: protection from eviction, harassment and excessive rents to name but three. A prospective landlord can find out his legal rights and duties from a solicitor or organization such as the Citizens' Advice Bureau. Generally, the 'closer' you are to a tenant – in other words if you provide breakfast, clean the room and do the laundry – the more control you, as a landlord, retain. On the other hand, if you let out the self-contained basement flat, for example, your new tenant may seek a rent reduction from the Rent Tribunal and be difficult to move as well. Many people co-exist with a lodger or two for years at a time, but since this is an area fraught with legal niceties it is as well to know where you stand before you begin.

Assuming you let out a room or two in your own home, you will have to decide exactly what kind of service you are going to provide and how much you are going to charge for it. Local experience is the best guide here. Judith R has let a couple of rooms to lodgers for several years and, on the whole, it has worked very well. Both rooms have wash basins and kettles and one has a cooker. One tenant has just left after seven years. Judith R cleaned the room and washed the sheets, and it has been an ideal and undemanding relationship. The other room has been occupied by a series of tenants; the rent recently went up to £7.50 plus an evening's babysitting. Now that her own family is bursting at the seams one of the rooms is being brought back as a children's bedroom. The other room will probably be let to a 'house guest', who has the run of the place and basic food supplies such as tea, milk and bread. Looking at the house as a whole, Judith R has found it important to 'know I can go into all the rooms in the house. Otherwise it would just be a number of split-up units.'

That is one way of doing it. Fred M has an entirely different arrangement. He saved up enough money to buy an eight-roomed house on four floors in 1968 and, being single, intended to keep three rooms for himself, let out four separate rooms to four people and share a communal kitchen. He fixed the plumbing, put in a shower, gas fires in each room and a coin telephone on the landing. Then he advertised for tenants in *New Society*. 'Without vetting people,' he says, 'I arranged it so those people came who I wanted: ex-sociology students and social workers.' In his case the primary motive for letting rooms was not so much the rent as 'the difference between living on my own in a bedsit to being with people'. 'Being with people' means 'sharing a kitchen with me, the landlord. I made sure that I kept more territory than anyone else because they are transient and anyway it's my house.' For all its informality Fred M's relations run smoothly with his tenants because, he suspects, both sides know what is expected of them. 'You have to know the limitations of the set-up,' he says, 'and you have to know what your real position is as a landlord. There's some flexibility but you can't demand too much.'

Despite his quip, 'I regard my tenants as walking pound notes,' Fred M charges well below market rents. 'In any case there is a wide band of market prices,' he says, 'depending on what is offered. I couldn't see myself living off rents because I wouldn't be prodded into doing anything.' Reasonable rents, he feels, are a key factor in peaceful relations. 'Rents are a heavy part of a person's income,' he says. 'If they are not a heavy part it makes a whole difference to the situation.' One side-effect of his renting policy is the reluctance of his tenants to leave. 'There are good reasons to leave after a while,' he says. 'People outgrow one room. I've got a feeling there are one or two dragging about leaving and letting the money factor weigh too much.'

Seven months later
'We've got no lodgers at the moment,' says Judith R. 'We've been decorating one of the rooms and in a couple of weeks the stair carpet will be down and then we'll see about it. I'm working in a playgroup four mornings a week and that gives me £14 a week clear.'

'My longest tenant has just left,' says Fred M, 'and I'm leaving the room empty for a bit while I see what happens. Apart from that, nothing new.'

Part-time
Capital: sufficient for the house in the first place
sufficient to equip room(s) with basic necessities like heating and furniture (if provided)
no separate premises
Income: A
Qualifications: none

Chapter Five
Children & Teaching

PLAYGROUPS

Katherine B clearly loves children. She has several of her own and, when they started going to school, 'I wanted a job where I would be free during the holidays and flexible,' she says, 'and be at home when they came back from school.' The local education authority was running a one day a week course for playgroup leaders and Katherine B went along. 'It was very good,' she says. 'It covered every aspect of running a playgroup. Many people started out with strange ideas of what children can do. You have to bring the ideas down to something very basic and simple.' The potential playleaders on her course were mainly other mothers, some of whom had previously trained as primary school teachers; there were also two nannies and one man.

While on the course, which lasted a year, Katherine B got a job as a helper with a playgroup in a tower block of flats. 'I put leaflets through all the doors advertising the playgroup and went up and down street markets talking to people and asking everybody with children if they would like to come to a playgroup. We had coffee mornings, all this sort of thing. It varies with the area you're in; in some areas you can't have a coffee morning, it's better to have a fish and chip evening.' Not many children came despite all the campaigning, so that playgroup was postponed. Then

Katherine B was asked to revitalize a rundown playgroup which had very little to offer the children except plasticine and a climbing frame. She went to work. With a group of mothers she organized a jumble sale. 'To my amazement we raised £100,' she says. 'We bought a very nice water trolley, a good, strong, large sand tray and some painting easels and paint. And we bought some books and some jigsaws and that's how we started.'

The playgroup movement has been gathering strength and new recruits in the last few years. It caters for three to five year olds, meeting in community centres, church halls, private homes or even converted builders' huts during weekday mornings. For many children, particularly in urban areas, it is the one opportunity 'to play with children of their own age,' says Katherine B, 'to sing rhymes, look at books, hear stories and play with water, sand, paint and clay'. For many of the children an attentive adult is the best company. 'Communication is very important to a lot of little children,' she says. 'A lot of parents don't actually talk to their children. I was staggered that even in the beautiful weather all they seem to do after playgroup is go home and watch television, day in, day out.' A playgroup will cater for about twenty children; there will be one adult in charge and a helper and, in well-run playgroups, a rota of mothers who volunteer to come in one day a week. 'We really want the mother to help,' says Katherine B. 'If she can't help on the rota, she can wash the painting aprons or make dressing-up clothes. I know a father who is very good at woodwork. Children can hear the radio or a record and they don't even start to think how it works. If somebody comes in and plays the guitar or the piano it makes all the difference. Or we get somebody from the Tufty Club to come and talk about road safety; they have films and puppets and that goes down very well.'

Katherine B is not self-employed at all. Her playgroup was run by the N.H.S. who paid her £1.50 an hour; other playgroups are organized under the umbrella of the Pre-School Playgroups Association. Running a private playgroup is no different from running any other except that there is more to do, more preparatory work before opening day. Any playgroup charging a fee must conform to health and fire regulations comparable to those required for child-minders. Children must also be insured. If a private house is used for a playgroup, planning permission will be needed for 'change of use'. The P.P.A. can help with advice and information on all these matters.

Playgroups vary a great deal in how much they charge; 50p seems reasonable, though there are some who charge less, some more. 'If you are running your own playgroup you can charge what you like and do quite well from it,' says Katherine B, 'though I wouldn't advise anybody to do it just for the money alone.'

Seven months later
'I think it should be emphasized that playgroups are not just for dumping children. The P.P.A. is very keen to keep the family together so that parents, grandparents, everybody helps with the playgroup.'

Part-time (mornings only in term-time)
Capital: about £100 for equipment
rent for separate premises or large spare room in private house
helper's wage £18 to £20
Income: A
Qualifications: course run by local education authority

CHILD MINDING

'Never in my wildest dreams', says Brenda W, 'had I thought of looking after another child.' Nevertheless, this is exactly what has happened. Madeleine has been coming to her in the afternoons for three months now, first on a trial basis and then until she starts school in September. It has been a great success. Brenda W's youngest daughter has someone of her own age to play with, Madeleine has entry to a happy home, her mother can go to work (which she was doing anyway) and Brenda W collects £10 a week.

She found her job pinned to a local noticeboard. 'I was hard-up,' she says, 'and looking for quite different work. I saw there was a child, three and three-quarters, who needed to be looked after and it just seemed the right thing to do, something I could do at home without leaving the children.'

Child minding has been strictly controlled by law since it was discovered that very many children were being minded in appalling conditions. Brenda W can look after one child in the afternoon on an informal basis. If she were to mind more than one, she would need to be registered with the local council. In that case 'you have to have the facilities. The fire officer comes round and checks all the installations and you have to put gates at the top of the stairs and wash basins the right height.' The registered child minder's name is added to local authority records and is also given to local doctors ('it is surprising how many women ask their doctor this sort of thing').

Child minding seems a comparatively simple way of making money, but that attitude has its own dangers – not least for the child – says Brenda W. 'It's easy to say, well, if you have one for £10 why not have six and it brings in £60 a week? The temptation is there. But the sort of child who goes to a child minder hasn't got its own mother, for whatever reason, so really they need individual attention, extra care.' And individual attention at 40p an hour is the going rate. 'I know my neighbour next door feels that it is a down-market occupation,' she says. 'Those that can't get another job do this. It had never occurred to me that it was thought of like that. Perhaps it is so, as people are only willing to pay you half or less what they pay you to clean their house. To take full responsibility for the influences on that child for 40p an hour!' From that point of view, it is small financial reward for work which is as potentially important as that of a teacher. From the working mother's point of view a full day's minding 'at 40p an hour is about £18 a week which may be half of that lady's take home pay. So you can see that the mother might be very tempted to use an unregistered child minder round the corner who is squashing six children into completely unsuitable premises.'

Brenda W looks after Madeleine as if she were her own child, perhaps even better, she says. 'I personally feel more responsible to Madeleine when she is here than I do to mine. If she cuts herself out playing I rush out with Dettol and plasters, whereas if its your own you assess it very quickly.' It is quite a responsibility, she admits. 'I think it must be stressed that unless you feel relaxed with your own children most of the time it isn't a job to do. I don't think it's a job to take on lightly. To be a mother at home with young children is difficult anyway; you've only got to look round a doctor's surgery at young mothers on Valium or Librium to see that. You have to be fairly easy-going because I could see how if you got extra tired or felt under pressure you would take it out on your own family.'

Six months later

Both Madeleine and Brenda W's youngest child are now at school, so Brenda is no longer child minding. 'I've become a landlady,' she says. 'I have a student lodger in the house from this week. He pays me £24 a week for bed and breakfast and an evening meal. He even paid me in advance! I also work as a mother's help for three hours every morning at £1 an hour. I could be doing anything. This morning I had to run her husband to the station and look for an antique lamp post on the way.'

Part-time
Capital: none

£1.50 a week for Madeleine's lunch
no separate premises

Income: A
Qualifications: none

TEACHING

i. Singing and music

Any student can have a hard time leaving college; all of a sudden the wraps are whisked away, and with little knowledge of the commercial world and less experience of earning a livelihood it can be a daunting business. A very few jet to the very top of their profession; some never try, but most put on their boots and settle down for a long haul. Rosemary B is one of these. She is a good pianist but, on her own admission, not good enough to play solo. Coming from New Zealand on an Arts Council bursary she studied at the Royal Academy for three years and then found herself without a job and with nowhere to go. 'I hadn't planned at all,' she says. 'You're not encouraged to if you're artistic, you're not supposed to worry about things like that; your great talent should see you through, something should come down on strings from heaven.' It didn't.

Fortified by twelve hours piano teaching at a school, just enough to live on, Rosemary B started giving one or two private lessons. 'I was living a nomadic life at the time,' she says, 'because I could never keep down any lodgings for long; I was carting this piano about. It was the noise really. The problem of a musician. You're too much in someone's private house unless they want it.' Then, about a year after she left college, Rosemary B began to play for an I.L.E.A. evening class. Her total earnings were £19 a week. Now, six years later, she gives twenty hours a week private coaching (and two or three children's piano lessons) at £2.50 an hour and spends another twenty hours playing for young aspiring professional singers in I.L.E.A. classes, principally Opera Viva. What has happened in the six years?

'I had to live so I had to work,' she says. 'I was moving in several different directions at once and not knowing where I was going, and I was green and as soft as a bag of sponges about money. It seemed demeaning one's art to be selling it for money and yet one wasn't good enough to perform. I should have realized that if I wasn't good enough to perform I was doing what was my level, teaching, but it took me a while to accept that. There was an Indian philosopher, once, who said, "You can only teach people what is already inside them." I read it in a little book. I think that in the performing arts to be told something is not very useful. What you've got to do is inspire the person to a level of response where they start to do things that are in them. Sometimes it's valid to say, "Do a *crescendo* on that note," because you can see that they have the germ of the idea in their mind and haven't dared to do it. I prefer to say, "It would be nice to do that . . . " so we arrive at it between us.

'With singers it's very interesting, because every voice has its own quality. You're not teaching them singing, they've got all the notes; you've got to start with the quality of that particular voice. It's absolutely fascinating because it's always different; sometimes I feel that I had a good session with so-and-so, I really got a response from them, I lifted them up to a level they wouldn't have got to on their own. That's what it is, you're really behind them, not in front, so they in the end go forward themselves . . . that must be the aim of all good teaching – that you're behind the students, propelling them forwards. In the end they'll have enough momentum in their own legs and they'll go away from you. It's very like being a good mother, being a good teacher. I've told you that great teaching is the best thing that can happen to art because it will raise the level of performance. Performers will teach each other, but if there are one or two to whom the top singers can go and learn something, they're the most valuable people in the singing profession. They're the ones who keep the art alive.'

Eight months later
'Well, nothing very much has changed except that the I.L.E.A. are paying more for Opera Viva which is nice.'

Full-time
Capital: none
no separate premises but room for piano
Income: C
Qualifications: from Royal Academy of Music

ii. English

The English language has never been so popular; for various reasons everybody wants to learn it and many people come to England to do so. The language schools are busy. Elizabeth R, however, teaches English at home. Most of her students are foreigners: businessmen, diplomats, students and children. Other children, with learning or emotional difficulties, are sent from a local school for individual tuition. Elizabeth R is well versed for such a task. Head of the remedial section of a school, and later equipped with a teaching qualification from the International Language Centre, she found herself at home with two young children and spare time. She approached a near-by language school who recommended her to students. That was eight years ago and, apart from an attempt to teach in a comprehensive school, Elizabeth R has taught at home ever since. That is the way she prefers it: adults in the morning, children in the afternoon, the occasional outside visit to a family in the evening – on average, twenty hours a week, an hour at a time, except during the school holidays. The number of hours swing up and down, nothing constant about it, but it suits her other commitments of running a home and looking after a family. Occasionally something goes wrong. 'The children were ill in bed one day,' she recalls. 'I had one student who was late and the builder tramping round at the same time. Another potential student came to see me to arrange times and the next student turned up early. The final flourish was one of the children getting up and being sick down the stairs.' Now that the family has moved to a new house, one room is set aside for teaching, complete with books, tape recorder, table and a seal of seclusion.

Students want all sorts of things from English but, principally, they want to understand and speak it. Elizabeth R teaches conversational English with basic grammar; another local freelance teacher takes those who want more formal work. It is the stimulus of so many different students which appeals to Elizabeth R; that and the necessity of constantly looking afresh at English and its meanings. Over cups of coffee students progress through the present, the continuous present, the interrogative and the negative, and are encouraged to talk from the start. No difficulty so far. The difficulty, or at any rate the part which is unusual, is the method of payment. Elizabeth R says, 'I don't want to know about money, I don't want to have anything to do with it. When people say, "How much do you charge?" I never say a flat fee. I always say, "How much do you think I'm worth?" which puts it back to them.' This method of settling fees has some interesting results. Some Iron Curtain nationals pay generously without further discussion; middle-class people round her way 'always insist on getting as much for their money as they can and the richer they are the less they pay. They always take ages to pay too.'

Ruby P is a teacher; she has taught part-time in the village primary school for over twenty years, ever since her youngest child was five. At that time schools were glad of part-time teachers, but at the moment even full-time teachers are being dismissed and there are certainly no jobs for part-time ones. There is another aspect to this picture of outsize classes and educational gloom: many parents are concerned about whether their children are being taught at all. Some are, some are probably not. Ruby P did a few weeks supply teaching at a local school; then, when she left, she was asked to tutor her hairdresser's son, age ten, who had got on so well with his new, albeit temporary, teacher. So for one hour on Saturday mornings Jonathan comes for his English lesson. It is a new experience for both of them. 'He's a nice, chatty little boy,' she says, 'not all that bright and not making much headway in his class, probably a bit lost in his big school. We do English, not maths at all because his maths is quite good and unless you're working with the teacher you can do more harm than good. It's his English which needs work. We cover basic grammar and we're reading a book and doing a lot of work with a junior dictionary.' Jonathan also has homework to do before his weekly lesson.

At the start of the next term Ruby P is contacting the head teachers of all the local primary schools, offering to individually tutor children for £2 an hour if any parents wish it. 'It's probably better to work with the schools if you can,' she says. 'It's more effective and the child benefits more.'

Seven months later
'I'm going back to work full-time,' says Elizabeth R, 'really for financial reasons. It was lovely working at home, a fun thing, while the children were little, but now I'm going to find a job. That's definite.'

Part-time (term-time)
Capital: none
tape recorder useful
no separate premises
Income: A
Qualifications: from International Language Centre
teaching employment

Three months later
'I've just finished three days supply teaching so I'm keeping busy,' Ruby P says. 'No more private pupils as yet,

but I'm getting known through the supply teaching so I shan't have to advertise.'

Part-time
Capital: none
no separate premises
Income: A
Qualifications: from teacher training college
teaching employment

Chapter Six
Crafts

POTTERY

Helen Y thinks it important to remember to 'see your craft in its historical context, not just for people of your generation and taste but to make use of anything which keeps the horizons wide and shows that you are not just this little person working away in a small workshop but part of a very big tradition'. For her, day-to-day pottery is domestic stoneware – plates, bowls, jugs, teapots, beakers – which she makes, fires and sells from her mews workshop. The workshop was chosen carefully, an inexpensive location near a well-heeled area, and bought on a nineteen-year lease with a legacy.

Before she gave up her job, Helen Y was a hobby potter. After a full-time two-year training course, and with a workshop newly equipped with kiln and extensive shelving and stocked with materials, she set to and finds that, 'I can still say the same things about the work after ten years as I could after six months. It's rather more than half on commission and it's very local. The orders come from neighbours and friends. At the same time I can say that the pottery made here has gone to every continent, bought by people walking by.' All the pots are sold from the workshop; for Helen Y this is the best and simplest way. 'There has never been a time when there has been nothing in the books,' she says. 'Or, if the orders are a bit thin, there are gaps in the shelves, the casseroles are out of stock or the teapots are out of stock.' She works from one order to the next. If friends ask, 'How long are you going to go on doing this?' she answers, 'Well, I've got orders for the next three weeks,' and so it continues.

How does she manage to work so consistently from year to year without restlessness or boredom? 'I think you have to work very directly towards the order that has been given you,' she says, 'and try to see, in a subtle way, what it is that the customer is hoping to get. We all feel, when we are working, that we want to do something more individual, but that has to work in conjunction with the commission. If you just work on steadily and keep that customer in mind that really helps through this situation of working on your own. I find work is much sweetened in the context of the person who is either going to buy or use the thing that you are making. It makes the work easier to know that standards are important, because if you lose interest in it yourself that's when the work becomes heavy.'

Regular working hours, says Helen Y, help her; more difficult to maintain when on one's own but necessary, she says. 'You have to be rather cunning, use any subterfuge to avoid bouts of depression, go out for a walk for quarter of an hour, listen to the radio or television for a bit, have lunch with a friend – and then come back again. It's a combination of being disciplined and keeping at it and yet being resourceful and willing to do something different.'

A work book helps to keep life orderly. She has the one book, fourteen inches by nine inches with spongeable hard covers. Orders are written at the back. Work is written in detail at the front and made up into one unit, i.e., the filling of the kiln which is about two to three weeks work. Notes about the firing of the kiln go in the same book and 'it is useful to keep these notes,' she says, 'particularly of glazes, recipes and the weights used in, for example, a set of teacups. Really it saves so much time in the end. Today I had to measure out enough clay to do eight plates of medium size. I got it out of the bin, weighed it up and there was literally no clay left over. It was exactly right.'

There is demand for her pots throughout the year, which increases at Christmas, slackens off in the New Year and picks up again at Easter. Helen Y has advertised in the past: in the borough guide, a handout at the cinema and, at Christmas, in the local newspaper. Now she relies only on her business card because 'people like to have something to show where the pot was made.'

Seven months later
'Nothing very different has happened since I last saw you.'

Full-time
Capital: £8,000 bought lease of workshop with flat above and basic equipment
electric kiln was £300
'Don't be put off by these figures,' says Helen Y. 'You can build a kiln with bricks and, if you work hard, build up your business step by step with almost no capital at all.'
Income: A
Qualifications: two years at Harrow Art School

KNITTING

Knitting has such a homey, plump image; not everybody remembers what a robust yet delicate craft it is. Barbara A chanced on knitting almost as a joke. After mending Middle-Eastern carpets for a year, she knitted a sleeping-bag for a baby. It was knitted to look like a carpet in pattern and colours. It worked; everybody was delighted.

Barbara A carried on mending carpets; then she bought a knitting machine for £100. 'The worst that can happen', she thought, 'is that I make some nice clothes for myself and the best that can happen is that I also make my money back.' She started to knit V-neck sweaters, scarves and hats, all to her own carpet designs. A year ago friends opened a clothes shop and asked her to supply it; knitting output has since trebled and Barbara A now employs five knitters and two sewer-ups. She does all the designing on computer punch cards which fit into the machines and control the pattern, colour changes and so on. Her out-workers are paid by the piece; it works out at about £1 an hour. She estimates the wholesale price this way: 'I start with how long the garment is going to take,' she says. 'Is it a big job, is it complicated, therefore relative to everything else how much should I pay? Then I weigh it and find out how much wool there is and find out how complicated the sewing-up is. Then I add on a percentage for myself and that is the wholesale price.' She knits very little now. 'You get spoilt,' she says, 'a bit lazy, just scribbling away patterns, but I wouldn't want to knit three cardigans in a row anyway.'

Besides designing and the occasional knit, Barbara A's job is to supply her out-workers with everything they need. 'I have a driver,' she says, 'who goes around.' It sounds very organized. 'Ye-es,' she says, 'it can sound that way, but downstairs there are two little bags which have to be delivered. There's two ounces of oatmeal wool that I have to send to one of my knitters because she's run out and the other one is ten ounces of willow and two ounces of something else and a punch card that I didn't have finished before.' Wool supplies are a problem. 'What I need is very difficult to find in the colours I want,' she says, 'because you might find the right weight and it will be bright red, bright pink or baby pink, white and black and school brown. The English colours are incredibly unimaginative. Wool is supposed to be traditional to England; it just isn't, there are a lot of synthetics.' After searching she found wool in the colours and quantities she wanted in Scotland and France.

The shop helps a good deal in feeding back information

of the 'sleeves are too short' kind. 'I spend a lot of time at the shop,' says Barbara A. 'This week I'm going to be here every day because someone wants to be measured for something, someone wants to discuss a new colour scheme or what would match a skirt they've bought.' Self-employed people sometimes prefer working on their own; Barbara A prefers company. 'I was going out of my mind through lack of stimulation when I was carpet mending,' she says. The shop provides a better balance.

Barbara A's approach would not suit everybody, because every knitter has a different way of working and a different market. Her clothes come under 'what is labelled the ethnic look,' she says, 'though I think I can survive after the ethnic look is over. I'm going to move away from it before it moves away from me; they know what sells in the shop and we're going to get some new designs together.' She admits to lots of mistakes. 'When the shop opened it was February and the fashion magazines say that people are buying for summer. So we threw together a summer collection which was a bit of a flop but the winter stuff went right on selling.'

Although she has been knitting since she was eight, Barbara A never treated it seriously. Her art school training did nothing to teach her otherwise. 'The American system of education is great for teaching people to dabble,' she says, 'and it convinced me that knitting was mundane and should be avoided at all costs, whereas it was obvious that was where I needed to go.' Coming to England on a working holiday she decided to stay, and the easiest way to stay was to be self-employed. As a matter of fact she started up a company, far too soon and probably unnecessary, she says, but 'it was interesting, it took on a personality of its own. I suddenly had to make a go of it, I had to do justice to this separate entity.'

Eight months later

'I've started exporting,' says Barbara A. 'I've got two clients in Germany. One of them came to the shop and asked me to supply her shop in Munich and the other one came to a show which friends were having. It's now about half my business. While not much has been sold in the shop over the summer I've been able to get on and supply my new clients. Exporting is not that difficult, it's done through an air shippers. I have to be a bit more careful with the invoices, get proof of V.A.T., that sort of thing.'

Full-time
Capital: £100 for knitting machine
out-workers £1 an hour
driver £10 for around fifty miles
no separate premises
Income: A/B
Qualifications: art school

SADDLERY

'What started me', says Paul D, 'was that I hadn't found a saddle I was comfortable on. I thought I would make a comfortable saddle. I did but I ended up selling it.' That was in the Camargue two years ago, while staying with his father, where there wasn't much else to do. A little previous experience in saddle repairs and skills in wood – cabinet making, antique restoration, instrument repairs – and in making leather handbags all contributed towards creating a saddle, but 'it's a matter of commonsense,' says Paul D. 'You take something apart and you can see how it is made. If you're observant you look at what you're doing and it's not so complicated. You can put something on a horse and see where it isn't fitting. It's like a shoe. There are certain tricks, obviously, as there are in anything. You have to know something about anatomy otherwise you can do a horse awful damage. You just learn by practising and talking to people.'

Paul D is currently working on two types of saddle: one

for disabled people and another, similar, for trekking. The saddles are still at the prototype stage. He has chosen a specialized field. 'The only way I can make a living', he says, 'is to do something which nobody else is doing.' It makes sense in an area where most standard English saddles come from Walsall and others are imported from places like Switzerland, Italy and the Argentine. There are a few craftsmen making made-to-order saddles, especially racing saddles, but the trees (the wooden base) are nowadays bought from wholesalers. Paul D makes his. 'In any case, Western saddles [which he also makes] can't be mass-produced. You have to make the tree and mould the leather before it is cut.' There are outlets, he says, which need developing. Film work is one. 'In films of jousting, for example,' he says, 'I've often seen them doing it on ordinary English saddles and that's not how it should be.'

Both his saddles for the disabled and the trekking saddles have been designed to clip together for ease of repair and should work well in theory – in theory because they have yet to be sold or commercially tested. There are various organizations which might be interested. 'All I can do is get the saddles photographed, make up a brochure and send it to them,' he says. At the rate of around two a week, or more if he works hard on several at a time, the saddles will retail at about £80, of which about £25 will be materials. It took some time to initially develop the patterns and moulds and at least one manufacturer has shown an interest in buying the patterns, but 'I'd be cutting my throat because I need an income,' he says. 'It's the ideal work for me; it's very relaxing and I'm quite a slow worker because I'm fairly meticulous.'

While the saddlery is getting going Paul D is working on other things: a bit of shop furnishing, a bit of sculpture. 'I'm quite multi-faceted,' he admits, 'and it's very awkward; you're going in all directions at once. Eventually I want to live on saddlery, but even then I shall be doing other things, simply because I get bored with any one thing. Being self-employed, it's really difficult to discipline yourself. I probably work as long hours as anybody but it's all spread around.' Another problem for him is organizing the selling side. He puts it this way: 'I make something and once it's finished I'm not interested in it anymore, it's served its purpose. I'd as soon give it away, which isn't very good business.' In France there was a buyer for every saddle he made before it was finished; he doesn't yet know about England.

Nine months later
'I've moved to Hampshire and I'm converting a barn into a workshop there. The trekking saddles are being sold to a trekking centre in the Camargue and a shop in Paris. The Riding for the Disabled Association in this country has no money to spare for the other type of saddle, but it has been taken up as a dressage saddle by a Spaniard breaking horses – again in the Camargue. French customs charge forty per cent duty on imported saddles but, even so, there seems to be a demand for them. I'm still under-capitalized and waiting for money from France so I can stock up on materials.'

Part-time
Capital: materials – saddle costs £25, Western saddle costs £90
workshop
Income: A/B
Qualifications: none

LEATHER

For Gary D, an Australian surfer and factory worker, leather work started in 1969 with an invitation from an American on the Queensland Gold Coast to 'come down here and help me out. I'll show you what to do, show you a way of living.' It was no apprenticeship that first year, but he learnt enough of the basic laws of working with leather ('what to do and what not to do') and techniques of buying hides and selling the finished bags and belts to bring him over to England.

In London, Gary D worked for six months with a leather company classifying and grading leather; then he took off for California and St Augustine in Florida. The American tradition of leather work is rich in techniques, styles and patterns and while he was making belts, watchbands, bags, hair-slides and wallets Gary D was also refining and developing his work. On one occasion, he recalls, he was told that "the belts are just great, but the rivets, you're not doing those properly, it spoils the whole thing". You do the whole belt perfectly and you come to the last part, just two little rivets and you mess those up, do one a little bit crooked, little things like that you remember, it makes the whole difference.'

Virtually all his work is for a tourist market and, back in England, he went down to Cornwall where he set up with a sandal maker in Newquay. 'It was very basic leather work,' says Gary D, 'no tooling or fancy work on the outside. They had leather uppers and tire soles and they were selling all right because they were long-wearing.' This arrangement went on for three years, Gary D introducing new work and new ideas. He would go down and 'work my butt off in the summer and in the winter you had enough money to last you, if you were lucky, to come back and set up the next summer'. Tourist work is usually seasonal and it suited Gary D; he would winter in Morocco, India and Ceylon – intensive spells of work seasoned with intensive spells of lotus living.

However, it couldn't last. The Newquay sandal maker took all his ideas and is now mass-producing; Gary D moved back to London, got married and asked a leather-worker friend in Australia to be his partner. 'London is the largest tourist attraction in the world,' he wrote. 'The economy isn't too good, but if you come over we'll get something going.' It was the summer of 1975 and they worked outside in the garden well into the evening; but that couldn't last and the search for a workshop began in earnest as the days got colder. Finding a workshop at the right price can be a tedious operation for urban craftsmen, but eventually Gary D and partner were offered space at Camden Lock rented from a silversmith. It costs them £3 a week each. This is how things stand at the moment, and they work throughout the week to produce enough for the weekend markets (see page 45). It's mainly belts since 'we've found these to be the most popular, the easiest to make and the fastest to make because we make everything by hand.' Despite a sour economic climate, their work has been selling well. Leather work used to be one of those crafts which flooded the market with badly made goods; not anymore, says Gary D. 'A lot of leather workers have quit, their work wasn't very good. After six years I know how to finish it off properly, which is where a lot of people fail. The cost of leather is going up and it is only those people who are doing a little bit extra who will survive.' Gary D has found his market and prices his goods carefully. 'People have a set amount of pounds they want to spend, that's about £3 or £4. So we keep ourselves in that bracket.'

During the day, Gary D works as a cashier for an advertising agency. The job serves a double purpose: it will enable him to get a mortgage for a flat he and his wife are buying and it gives him a practical insight into how a small business is run. An evening class in accountancy and book-keeping tops up that side of things.

Eight months later

'I've been working full-time at the workshop since April, given up the job, and it's going pretty well; going up and down a lot, I only made 31p last week! On another week I might make £200. We've given up Portobello Road but we still go to Petticoat Lane and another market in the city,

St Christopher's Place, three times a week. Belts are still our main line, but we make anything useful in leather: bags, passport pouches, wristbands and custom-made sandals. We're really working seven days a week.'

Full-time
Capital: rent of workshop £30 a month (new rates)
tools worth about £800 between the two partners
Income: B
Qualifications: none

CLOTHES DESIGN

John D and his wife Molly work tucked into a prefab workshop away from the main commercial world, so 'we only see those people who really want to see us,' they say. They make silk-screened clothes: waistcoats, jackets, T-shirts, 'celebrating in print the things we come across', whether it's fat strawberries, neon lights, tattoos or exploding martinis. Molly D's mother makes up the T-shirts and other friends help with sewing up the clothes, which are sold to manufacturers and fashion houses all over the world. Not everybody wants, or can afford, their clothes, but those who do are enthusiasts. Selling is the least of their problems; not that they have so many problems, their work is in great demand, but as John D says, 'If you create a demand it's your responsibility to supply it,' and that sometimes means a seven-day week.

Their problem is how to stay 'small and steady'. In their three or four years of full-time silk-screening they have received special offers from the *Sunday Times* and several companies coming to them with massive orders. 'Avoid it like the plague,' says John D. 'It means getting a huge overdraft, employing lots of people; avoid getting too big.' Then there are those who would like to buy them up and 'that's very dangerous,' adds Molly D. 'Those sort of people collect people, use them up and throw them away. That's one thing we've always steered clear of.'

Leaving art school with fine art and textile experience, they both taught and Molly D did a few prints and clothes while John D painted, sculpted and did illustration work. Then five years ago, they landed a workshop space with other artists and craftsmen and started work there. 'It was the first time we had a chance to set up a print table,' says John D. 'Before that we had a big dining table and a couple of blankets. We started printing things we had ideas for, peddled them around and sold them.' After a while offers started coming in and they dropped their other work and concentrated on printing 'because that's the one that took off'. Molly D designs the clothes and they both design the prints; they run them for as long as there is a demand, perhaps two thousand finished articles or twelve thousand. Molly also has the children to care for; the two eldest go to school and she brings the youngest to the workshop. They are buying a maisonette at the back of the workshop to make home/work organization easier.

The workshop itself is run as a co-operative trust; about half the artists/craftsmen rarely use it and that 'has affected the work of other people', says John D. 'Anybody who wanted the space could have it, which was a mistake because there are a lot of people for whom it has been a pipe dream. It takes weeks to arrange a meeting and then you never get a total decision.' This run-down is going to be halted, they say; apart from anything else they are applying for a new lease from the council, so everything must be thriving and vigorous.

John and Molly D intend to go on as before, perhaps taking up work in the States, perhaps making a film, perhaps not. 'It's all circumstantial', says John D; 'when the circumstances are right, you do something, right?' He is sceptical about an approach which says, in advance, 'I have decided to do this or that and I am going to earn a living from it.' The 'what can I do?' attitude, he says, does not work. 'Let's put it this way. If you want to go into silk-screening as a livelihood, choose something else. But if you want to get into it because you're interested in print and you just want to experiment and then, later, if you're lucky . . . that sort of approach, yes. Start on the kitchen table, it's easy. It only costs £30 to get the equipment together. I do think if you can find a way of working on your own, go out of your way to do it; it's much better even if you fail.' John D says that he couldn't give advice. 'I would say, "Don't give advice, go your own way." I'd give practical help but you can't give advice, everyone's lifeline is different.' For the two of them success is 'getting your life together to make your life work for you' and 'anyway you can't tell when you've got it'.

Eight months later
The workshop has been re-organized, the maisonette is bought, but 'we didn't go to the States,' says John D. 'For the last five months things have been really happening and all my little plans for getting out of the doldrums, like going to the States, I've just left those. We're bringing in a new table and designing quilts, bed quilts. The first one will commemorate the first British Beatles Convention and then we'll see.'

Full-time
Capital: for a beginner £30 to £40 covers basic equipment
separate working premises
out-workers paid by piece according to skill and complexity of garment
Income: C (each)
Qualifications: art school for seven years (John D in fine art; Molly D in textiles)

MUSICAL INSTRUMENTS

Michael S had a saw and a plane when he first started to

make lutes. There was no money to spare from his factory work so he went to a demolition site and picked up enough wood for a bench. A bending iron – for bending the ribs of the lute – was made from an old electric fire which someone had thrown out. 'I didn't spend any money on equipment at all,' he says. 'I just improvised.'

The sound of Renaissance music – 'It has a still quality' – together with the wish for his own business came together in an instrument – the lute – and then, later, rebecs and baroque guitars. A sculptor by training Michael S had very little experience with wood, but 'when I was younger I had the feeling that I could do anything I wanted to do if I put my mind to it and it seemed a relatively easy job to make a musical instrument.' Basically, he says, 'one has to be able to cut a straight line and plane a flat surface, to do some cutting with a knife, carefully, for example with the rose, understand something about volume and to be able to visualize how things go together.' After seeing a lute at a concert for the first time, another lute maker introduced him to the techniques of making a lute from beginning to end. With an instrument in his hands, he drew it and constructed his own. Another lute followed, which found its way to Canada, and Michael S stopped work at the factory. It was 1971.

Anybody, so he says, can make a musical instrument of sorts; it is the sound which emerges from it which distinguishes one craftsman from another. 'It's the tensions and pitches which have evolved,' he says. 'I suppose I have quite a good ear for listening because that's all one needs to have. I don't even play a lute very well. It's the technicalities which one has to get over initially. You can't learn from books. The only thing to do is go ahead; the more you do it the more you understand it is like it is and what is needed.'

Musicians make a very discriminating market, found partly through advertising but mainly through reputation. Beginner makers sell mostly to beginner players and then a lute, moderately priced, would fetch around £250 to £300. Lutes sold abroad can be double the U.K. price. Most lute makers have a long waiting list. 'What happens', says Michael S, 'is that you start off with an order, then two orders and then the waiting list is six months, then a year, then four years. Now while all those people are waiting for lutes, and are prepared to wait, there are other people eagerly trying to get hold of lutes, so they go to new makers who have a waiting list of two months.' So it continues. It takes about a month to make a lute 'with all the bits and pieces one has to do, buy materials, answer the phone and deal with Fred who wants to come round and talk about lutes for three hours'. Lots of people want to talk about lutes. Early music is on a revival and good instrument makers are in demand. It takes time to develop the essential skills and not everybody can afford the wait; Michael S restored his workshop two and a half years ago with another lute maker who has since left. 'He couldn't keep going,' says Michael S, 'because he had three children and a wife to support. He started after I did but I feel that if he had carried on he might be all right now, but it wasn't secure enough at the time.'

The workshop is currently occupied by himself, another lute maker and, starting the following week, a keyboard instrument maker. They share the rent and some of the equipment. 'He uses my circular saw and I use his G-clamps every now and again,' says Michael S. Other tools, such as hole cutters and peg sharpeners, they make themselves. 'We make them all the time,' he says,' usc them for a while, they get worn out, so we make another.'

Nine months later

'As more information on old lutes becomes available,' says Michael S, 'I'm finding that our discoveries are becoming an integral part of making new ones. It's a matter of refining details: woods, pegs, thicknesses, string tensions, spacing. There's also a new workshop opened next to the Music

Centre and there are five extra people making musical instruments. It's really good to work with others; we pass on information and we've just bought our first load of wood together.'

Full-time
Capital: none at beginning
tools cost £800 (including grindstone, bandsaw, circular saw and planer)
cost of making one instrument £30 to £40 (soundboard £10, pegs £12 to £15, strings £8)
instrument case costs £54
rent of workshop £30 (shared between three)
Income: C
Qualifications: none

PICTURE FRAMING

What can you do if you don't have a job and you can't speak the language too well? 'I didn't know what to do,' says Christian G. 'I had always wanted to work with my hands and one day a friend said, "Why not try picture framing?" [which he did]. I was hesitating between picture framing and book binding and I found the picture framing work first.' Apprenticed to an old-established picture framing firm for two and a half years, Christian G learnt the fundamentals of his craft including gilding. He recommends an apprenticeship: 'You are always learning, especially in restoration. You can spend six months on a course and you know the rudiments, but you've got to work on different jobs over a period of time to know what to do.' He adds, 'I thought I was very clumsy before I started this work.'

Seven months ago he set up on his own in partnership with the foreman of the firm. 'He is coming at night and on Saturday,' says Christian G, 'and I hope that in six months or a year we will be able to work full-time together.' Work has been no problem. Perhaps they have been lucky. In any case, when a gallery asked them to supply frames for pictures in the World of Islam festival they were ready. A friend makes most of the frames and Christian G does the gilding. He charges £2.50 an hour and works, on average, about six hours a day. 'I am interested in the money,' he says, 'but it is not the main thing. To be able to work when I wanted to, two hours a day or even at night – that was the main thing.' It is a little soon to say how the work will eventually stabilize. Christian G knows the direction he would like to go: 'Simple framing, especially classical or restoration framing,' he says. It is not only a craft in itself; the picture framer also needs to know about painting and a bit about furniture.

Besides gallery connections, many picture framers take in work from the general public. Gallery work, however, is better paid. 'I am not expensive,' says Christian G, 'but I am charging a fair price because I do more work than a normal picture framer.' His prices are still less than West End framers, largely because his overheads are much lower. 'The galleries go to these picture framers,' he says, 'but the price is too high for them. That's how I get my deal.' Then, 'you have to have a competitive price. If you are too expensive you are not going to get work, especially if you have a small workshop and you have no name. To establish a picture framing business you have to work from mouth to ear, it takes quite a long time.'

Christian G found it easy to start his workshop. In Paris, he says, it would have been much harder, much more expensive to find a place to work. In England, he says, 'if you know your trade and have a bit of money on your side, you can start like that with no official permission, no permit.' He had no money at all but borrowed £2,000 – more than enough – 'because I wasn't expecting work to come so quickly. I spent about £900 on buying equipment and on key money which was £250.' A major outlay is £300 a month on gold leaf. 'I get it back but I need that amount.

If I didn't have the money,' he says, 'I would go to a gallery, because there are few people doing gilding apart from the established firms, and ask them to lend me some money while I was working for them. I am sure this kind of thing is possible.'

Six months later
'I am working for two galleries,' says Christian G, 'the one I first mentioned and now another one. There is a lot of work and it is going very well, which is good because I have just bought a house.'

Full-time
Capital: £2,000
equipment cost about £650
rent of workshop £69 a month
Income: C
Qualifications: apprenticeship

MODEL SHIPS

Some people have hobbies; others, like Jonty T, have model-making. 'It grips you,' he says. At the age of seventeen he gave it up. 'I can remember it,' he says, 'a conscious decision that it was too private, too inward-looking.' Now, twenty years later, restoring and rigging model ships is half his livelihood. The other half is graphic design. Both activities are doing well. In graphic design he has got to the point where he can choose the bigger, fruitier jobs, but model ships are also on the increase, either battered hulks requiring a complete overhaul or sleek hulls needing a canopy of rigging. He will take any type of sailing ship: waiting in his workshop were a modern Greek yacht and a number of tiny wood and bone ships made by Napoleonic prisoners-of-war.

In 1967 model ship restoration took off for Jonty T; the first was a ship in a bottle belonging to his parents-in-law and then others came in through the Parker Gallery. 'I could do one,' he says, 'take it up, bring back another one, do it in a few weeks, take it up.' Most of it was restoration work; in addition, 'there was an old boy in Lancashire who used to make nice hulls, but he wasn't interested in masting and rigging, the string bit. I used to get these almost perfectly finished hulls and do all the masting and rigging.' The supply of beaten-up ships flows on. 'I've gone through the first phase one seems to go through,' he says, 'of (a) finding out what one can do and (b) living through one's dreams of what one wants to do. This slightly antiquey, craftsmanship type, I'm beginning to realize it more and more, that really is me. It's beginning to gel.'

Ship models are, of course, only one tributary of a whole stream of modelling. Jonty T also makes chess figures. 'I've done a little work, and there is probably more if I could find it, replacing chess figures, little oriental pieces. They're generally carved in ivory. I replaced them in holly wood which is almost dead white and very, very hard.' Then there is heraldry: 'I painted a coat of arms on a coach just before Christmas.' Isn't that very specialized? 'You have to do a bit of research, but I've got a continuing interest in history,' he says.

Despite other interests, Jonty T loves ships the best. 'The shape of the hull is so beautiful,' he says. 'It's total economy, a balance between wind and water, nothing superfluous except perhaps the scrolling round the figurehead.' He describes his approach to the work. 'It's highly technical and highly detailed. I sometimes feel akin to the dentist, I think we're in similar lines of business. The detail is just a certain sort of richness. It takes so long to do. You end up with a whole and the richness of the whole is due to the fact that it's full, it's completely composed. There are countless little bits and pieces which, though they're pretty unimportant in themselves, they're so small, you've put in maximum effort to every little piece and it builds up. The total is greater than the sum of its parts because of the concentration and energy.'

Since he is at the stage where he can choose his work, especially with graphics, what will he choose? Where can he go from here? 'I now want to progress; which means money and expansion, and there are various options. One has either got to become a small business, no longer a one-man show, but get a partner with some capital, or, if you're not going to do that, you yourself have got to make yourself bigger and better because you're the product in a sense.' He has chosen not to become a businessman because 'I would have ended up behind a desk,' but to take the other path, 'in musical terms becoming a soloist rather than staying in an orchestra. I found that by aiming relatively low you don't take the risk of being rejected, but you get to the stage where you've classed yourself low on the professional ladder and therefore the financial returns are relatively low. O.K. you're super-efficient, you get it all done and you get a living at the end of the month, but you can't get any further because there isn't time, the wheels are spinning so fast, you can't do things on spec. I'm currently at the point of climbing out of that one.'

Seven months later
'In the next month I'm working on more ships coming from the Greeks; I've also contacted a dealer in ship's models and work may be coming from that. I've written an article on restoration for *Model Shipwright*, it's a good quarterly magazine. Really, things are continuing to get better.'

Part-time
Capital: tools cost about £200, of which the most expensive piece of equipment is a lathe, £100
no separate premises; one room used as workshop
Income: B
Qualifications: none

Chapter Seven
Eating & Entertaining

RESTAURANT

Stephen J and his sister are running a wholefood snack bar in a university students' union. It is an *ad hoc* arrangement whereby they have the usè of a large room with serving area and a back room with washing-up sinks. 'The rest we had to find ourselves,' he says. 'We needed an oven, a fridge and something to boil the water up. The union financed these to the tune of £300 since we couldn't afford them straight off.'

Five months ago Stephen J gave up a teacher training course to work with his sister, a wholefood cook of five years standing; their only previous 'restaurant' experience was running a couple of stalls at pop festivals. With only three weeks to go before opening, they worked non-stop to get everything ready in time. Their list of essential jobs included: installing the cooker, buying crockery from jumble sales and second-hand shops, fitting locks on the doors, working out a menu, getting entry to a couple of cash and carrys (essential for bulk supplies of everything from cheese to plastic cups), stocking up on everything they could possibly need, ordering milk and bread and distributing small publicity posters. One day was spent finding and negotiating supplies from a greengrocer in the market. Food also came from a wholefood supplier in the town.

Chairs and tables were a problem; they made do with the low tables and easy chairs already there. A van they already had and this, Stephen J says, is essential.

With everything ready they were in business. The first to come were the faithful organic few, 'members of the Whole Earth group,' says Stephen J, 'who were pretty disgruntled about the university food'. The word spread that there was good food, music and a room with a view and now about two hundred people eat there every week. The snack bar, which is open over lunch-time during term, is manned by Stephen J and his sister and part-time student help. They have recently changed over to self-service because 'the queues were getting so ridiculous people had to wait twenty minutes before they got served. Self-service is a pretty miserable way of doing it but it's really efficient. It usually runs with two people behind the main counter doing hot foods and making sure all the salads are topped up, one person doing drinks – tea, coffee, fruit juice – and one person taking money at the end.'

Vicky J does all the cooking, mainly to her own receipes; the food includes well-tried favourites such as soups, vegetable stews, cauliflower cheese, savoury flans, apple pie, fruit cakes and specialities like giant cookies. Prices work out at the cost of the food plus sixty per cent to cover expenses such as the van, wages and rent. 'It seems to be a pretty good formula,' says Stephen J. 'People are happy to come along and pay the prices and we're quite happy with the money that is coming in. It was a bit low at first, but now more people are coming in.' Prices, though, are a contentious issue between him and some members of the union. Although their food is cheaper than cafés and vegetarian restaurants in the town, it is more expensive than the bar downstairs which also offers food and than the snack bar upstairs which is run by the university at a loss and subsidized. But, says Stephen J, 'we're not prepared to run at a loss and ask somebody to subsidize us. Our argument is that if you don't like the prices you don't buy the food. If you don't buy the food we go out of business.'

When the lunch-time rush is over, most of the baking is done for the next day, so they usually finish around five or six unless they are catering for an evening function, such as a society's meeting. Most of the food buying is done at the weekend. 'That's one of my jobs,' says Stephen J, 'to drive the van and pick up all the supplies. Friday night is usually down to cash and carry to stock up for the next week. Saturday morning we stick in an order with the greengrocer and pick it up in the afternoon. It's surprising how much work it takes, mainly because there are only two of us.'

Part of the work is peculiar to their surroundings. Since they share a washing-up room with the bar everything has to be moved around and out again the next morning, especially after concerts or discos. The health inspectors from the local council are interested in all these arrangements and one of them came down a couple of weeks ago to look over the premises. 'You've got to have a reasonably clean set-up,' says Stephen J, 'and they look for first-aid boxes, clean floors, there's got to be no animals, insects or mice around. There are a few things he pointed out which we'll have to get over – one of these is glass shelving for covering the food.' Stephen J cannot just go out and 'buy shelving, it's too expensive. But they're reasonable people, they'll give us a fair time to do it and then come back and inspect.'

Health inspections aside, one of his irritations is the union or 'squabbles with the lefties' as he calls it. 'They don't like to see private enterprise going on under their noses. They want to know how much control they have over us and on the profit we're making.' As he sees it, if he drops his prices he either goes out of business like the vegetarian place downstairs which ran at a loss and left the union with a bill or he gets subsidized, which he is unwilling to see happen. 'The food has to be paid for in the end,' he says.

It is a complaint against him which has nothing to do with him personally or the standard of the food, but much more with the fact that he is working for himself. Whether they stay or go 'depends on who gets in power next year. We're not interested in letting anybody control us, we'll just leave.'

Six months later
During the summer vacation the university union asked Stephen J to submit a tender for the snack bar. In the end the union did not accept it. Then, two weeks into term, they offered the snack bar back to Stephen J. Meanwhile Vicky J had a job and he had a thriving business importing and distributing board games (another earlier interest). They might take up the offer, but everything is undecided at the moment.

Full-time (during term-time)
Capital: none
outlay on food £100 to £150 per week
casual help 50p to 60p an hour
£10 a week rent (approximately)
van essential
Income: A; other income from record stall, disco and importing board games
Qualifications: catering skills

PUB

'How about a pub when we retire?' Not a good idea, according to Michael K, the landlord of a pub in Oxford. Perhaps there are pubs down country lanes suitable for elderly but active couples, but on the whole pub life is as strenuous as any other, requiring considerable reserves of energy and stamina. 'Horses for courses' is a phrase which seems to fall off the tongue of anybody connected with the brewery trade: there's a pub for you if you can find it. Michael K found his after he and his wife looked at 130 others. 'There are many ways to go about getting a pub,' he says, 'but we went to a broker. As we didn't know anything about pubs we spent a long time looking at pubs all over the country. It was a useful exercise; the more we saw, the more we learnt.' They applied for three tenancies: the first one, in the wilds, would never have given them a living; the second one they missed through lack of experience; but the third one was just right – the brewery wanted a tenant with experience of students and Michael K has previously owned and run hostels for students.

Now with his wife, daughter, son, son-in-law, parents and staff he is running a large and busy pub. For the first four and a half years it was a tenancy, tied for supplies to one brewery; then Michael K bought the freehold from the brewery who were having distribution difficulties. Now it is a free house. What makes a good pub? Michael K is certain that 'it's a meeting point, a safety valve, people come to talk. When the door opens you've got to be ready, you've got to be ready to serve them. That's what it is about.' A lot of preparatory work goes on before the doors open. At half-past eight in the morning, he says, 'we talk about what we require in the way of food, what we need to buy. Then we get down here, let the staff in and if, like yesterday, I was minus four staff I have to start cutting sandwiches instead of going to the office.' At half-past ten the pub opens until half-past two; then there is a short breathing space until six, when it opens again until half-past ten or eleven on Fridays and Saturdays. After the last customer has gone there is still clearing up to be done. Most of the customers are students, college servants, workers from Cowley and, in the summer, tourists at lunch-time. It is a mixed group which seems to gel together, he says; the odd truculent one is dealt with by his wife. 'She handles the odd awkward customer very well,' he says, 'better than if I approached him.'

Michael K is fortunate in that he has a lot of family help. His wife and daughter do the cooking (cold buffet at lunch and grills in the evening), his son buys the wines, his son-in-law looks after V.A.T. and similar duties and his parents are there in the morning. 'It makes it a lot easier for me because I can have holidays,' he says, 'which a lot of publicans can't.' The catering side needs a lot of work. 'Food fluctuates so much,' he observes, 'that it is more difficult to handle than the wet side; it needs a lot of homework keeping up with the prices. Basically it comes down to portion control.' Although his pub is large, the same principle applies to any other pub which offers food. 'You have to suit your catering to the requirements of your customers,' he says. 'When we came here it was rather expensive so there wasn't much catering. We provided a cheaper meal and that did the trick.'

Although Michael K had no previous experience of pubs, he recommends working in one for both husband and wife before committing themselves. 'It's a lot harder than many people think,' he says, 'both physically and mentally. It can be demanding on family life, especially with young children.' Having decided that this is what they want, there are still a number of pitfalls which the brewery will point out at the interview for a tenancy. The chief of these is money. Buying a free house can cost from £27,000 to £30,000 upwards and even a tenancy is not cheap. The premium, a deposit which is held until the pub is vacated, can cost from £500 to £1,000 depending on turnover; ingoings, everything from lightbulbs to chairs, can either be a small amount or up to £10,000; working capital is also needed. Having found a tenancy, the new publican is very much his own boss in the day-to-day management of the pub within a broad framework laid down by the tenancy agreement. The brewery will inspect the premises now and again, especially for cleanliness. 'Cleanliness', says Michael K, 'is all-important. You have to clean everything religiously otherwise the beer is not going to be good. That is essential.'

Full-time
Capital: free house £27,000 to £30,000 upwards
ingoings £10,000 or less
tenancy premium from £500 to £1,000
one full-time barman £40 to £50 a week
family assistance
Income: C
Qualifications: none

DISCOTHEQUE

Peter B loved parties and rock music and this prompted him to devote £2,500 plus two years of evenings and weekends to researching, developing and building a discotheque and lighting system. It was originally intended to fit into a large suitcase. In practice it occupies a transit van and requires three-quarters of an hour and two strong men to set it up. It has cost him many friends (and many parties) through neglect and will never, he says, financially repay him. So why did he do it? 'It was just the interest of designing this mammoth thing,' he says, 'that eventually took over my life. It started when I was about eight or nine; my parents' record player went wrong several times and I put it right. I sang in a choir and when my voice broke I collected albums and started building my own equipment. In the end I had to build a good disco just to satisfy myself.'

With no specialized knowledge of electronics, but with years of information garnering behind him, Peter B set to work. He decided on records rather than tapes (he had one hundred L.P.s at the time) and started the long haul of adding, subtracting and combining equipment until he arrived at the right sound. 'With a discotheque,' he says, 'you have to combine reliability, ruggedness, quality and portability. All these things are needed.' This is what his publicity brochure says:

Belt drive decks are employed for their low rumble

factors.

Magnetic cartridges with elliptical stylii are mounted in low mass–low friction arms to ensure optimum tracking.

The signals are then (RIAA) equalized and passed to the mixer which has comprehensive tone controls.

The mixer feeds the quadrophonic decoder and the final amplification is made through transistorized low distortion high power slave amplifiers.

The front speakers are transmission line enclosures each incorporating four units separately fed from high quality cross-over filters.

Rear speakers are omni-directional quarter wave folded horn types with good dispersion properties.

'I built everything twice,' says Peter B, 'because things were either too heavy, too big, too small or didn't work. It's important to be able to update; very rarely do people get it right first time unless they've got endless amounts of money.'

For the timid there are other ways of setting up the hardware: buy a proprietary system (£100 to £800 without lighting); buy parts from different systems to get a suitable combination; buy a second-hand system from retailers or watch *Exchange & Mart*. Before buying anything check it over thoroughly. Read hi-fi magazines. With a little woodworking ability a good alternative to D.I.Y. is to buy the separate parts and construct matching cases. Whatever is chosen will have to fit into a small area for private parties as well as catering for a larger space. Peter B aims to be adaptable. For a recent party he only used part of his equipment in a smallish room. Lastly, the most important part, he says, is to look after the records.

Now that Peter B has completed and tested the equipment, he has to sell the product. To date he has had three gigs, all friends, and the disco has worked perfectly. He has advertised in *Time Out*, *Melody Maker* and *Record Mirror* and will then advertise in the up-market *Harper's and Queen.* It is obviously evening work and his prices run from £10 to £15, depending on what people can afford; that price has to cover expenses such as petrol and insurance.

For the moment, at least, Peter B will continue working as an engineer during the day and join the eight to ten thousand part-time disco operators in the country. 'I've had a couple of offers to take the disco to Germany,' he says, 'but it means amazing insurance problems. The other thing I could do is to go into a town with a lot of young people, hire a hall, charge 30p or 40p a head, do a Friday and Saturday night show and move on.'

Seven months later
During the summer Peter B has been working a disco on riverboats up and down the Thames. 'It's a well-trodden course,' he says, 'but it only lasts during the summer. I've discovered that advertising is not worthwhile. Now I intend to contact all the local and sports clubs within a fifteen-mile radius, that's about four to five hundred clubs, offering regular gigs at their social and fund-raising events. For anybody starting out I've also discovered that it's much better to begin very simply, just as you would with hi-fi, and then add on as you need it.'

Part-time
Capital: £2,500 on equipment
van essential
no separate premises
Income: A
Qualifications: none

PUPPETRY

A man who has had sixty different jobs in his life, Derek C intends to play Punch and Judy until he is ninety. He grew towards puppetry after ten years acting and it developed from making his first papier mâché puppets to putting on shows in the Edinburgh theatres. Then, while acting in a dreary pantomime season, he said to himself, 'I shall never take on another part which I don't want to do,' and that decision, he says, was a big step. 'I didn't know how I was going to live, how I was going to support myself. I had started the Punch and Judy and was getting the odd booking. I became self-employed. As an actor one is always self-employed but this was different; I had to start learning how to promote myself, get shows together, write scripts and so on, things which I had never done.' Derek C kept the Punch and Judy show and developed others, including one called *Tales of King Arthur* which was written by his girlfriend. He discovered, not for the first time, that puppetry needed all his skills: 'Carpentry, tailoring, sculpting, everything came into making this production,' he says.

Although he is still taking the occasional acting part, Derek C is committed to puppetry. 'It can show all things at once,' he says. 'With Punch and Judy there are sixteen characters that I use. It's like the Tarot cards, they're aspects of yourself. Punch is the male aspect, Judy is the female aspect. It's a very moral tale; its roots lie right back in the mummers' plays.'

Now living in London Derek C has to start afresh, building up new contacts. 'As a performer you have to be seen,' he says, 'otherwise you don't work.' He plays to both adult and child audiences, but his favoured age group is the three to five year olds. 'The enjoyment comes from the less sophisticated part of the mind,' he says, 'and I've discovered that working with children because they respond immediately.' London is rather overstocked with puppeteers, he finds, and his fee has dropped from a dependable £20 to as little as £15. Apart from theatre bookings Derek C busks on the streets and entertains for birthday parties, pre-school play-groups and community groups, anywhere where there is an audience. He makes puppets for sale and teaches in children's workshops. In the summer Derek C and his dog will tour parks in Glasgow, Edinburgh and Dundee, playing from his purpose-built van. 'The idea of the show is that you're complete,' he says. 'I arrive and the show can start the second I get there. The van has a power supply, I can eat and sleep in it. It has two tape recorders, lighting and a drop-down stage. It's an old system, working out of doors in parks. You're competing with traffic, road drills and all sorts of distractions, but it's very rewarding because you get a mixed audience.'

In Edinburgh he was working with others; now he is virtually on his own and at times it is quite a strain. 'I find discipline is difficult to find,' he says, 'and difficult to maintain. You've got to be infinitely variable and resilient. If you can't paint the van because it is raining you've got to come in here and do something else. You can waste an awful lot of time worrying what to do instead of getting on with it.' Another thing, he says, is that 'if you're on your own you're constantly drawing on your own resources; you write the play, direct it, produce it and publicize it.' Once, after a depressing period without bookings, he went round to the labour exchange looking for a job – any job – but he discovered 'there is no way back. Once you know what you want to do, and I believe most people know, you just follow that.'

Six months later

'The Scottish tour went well,' says Derek C. 'I did seventy-five shows in six weeks. I'm soon off to South Hill Park community arts centre for six months where I'll be part of a little company of three people who I worked with in Edinburgh. We'll be "actors and actresses in residence", I think we are called. We shall be doing cabaret, pub shows and some puppetry. I hope to get a show of *Under Milk Wood* organized; it will be a big job, there will be fifty to sixty puppets.'

Full-time
Capital: one puppet costs about £1.50 to £2
van essential; equipped as 'theatre' costs £400
no separate premises
Income: A
Qualifications: skills in acting, sculpting, tailoring, carpentry

Chapter Eight
Services

HAIRDRESSING

People are very fussy about their hair and the way it is cut. They can be even fussier about who cuts it. A good haircut makes all the difference. Sharon M cuts hair at home. Trained on a six-month course with Vidal Sassoon, she worked in the salon for a while, then left to make wigs and work as a secretary – having nothing to do with hairdressing at all, except when friends came for haircuts. Three years ago one of them said, 'Why on earth don't you do freelance work?' so she did. 'When I started,' she says, 'I advertised in *Time Out*, which seemed to bring in the right type of people, people who didn't like going to salons, being pushed around, not given proper attention, all the hustle and bustle. Some people rather like that, others don't like it at all.'

Sharon M still advertises, but most of her clients now come by word of mouth. 'It's very enjoyable from that point of view,' she says. 'I probably know many of my clients quite well and that takes a bit of time to build up.' Advertising can have its problems. 'You can get some very strange phone calls,' says Sharon M, 'so I put "genuine callers only" and that cut down most of the odd people. You need an intercom system on the door at least so you can sound people out. If you're a woman and you're dealing with men you've got to be very careful. It depends on your attitude.

If you keep at a distance you're fine, I don't think there's any problem.'

Initially, Sharon M relied on an answering service which, as well as protecting her from unwelcome phone calls, 'had a diary for me so they made all my appointments; that was marvellous because it meant that I didn't have to discipline myself, I was almost being run by my agent'. Now married and about to move to a new flat, Sharon M is making her own appointments in a different market. She is hoping to reduce the number of individual clients and make visiting family appointments instead. 'I'm trying to set up home visits,' she says, 'going out to people, the woman at home with children who can't get out to the salon. After a time you get fed up being in the same place all the time and it's good for me because it means I can get out. I had a family yesterday, two next door neighbours and two children. So I did the four of them in one go.' Her new flat has a spare room which 'I'm going to turn into a salon with a proper floor, a basin in there so I can shut the door on it. You really need to. With people walking round you don't feel as if it's your home anymore.' For all that, a simple wash, cut and blow dry – which is what Sharon M gives – needs little space or equipment: scissors, brushes, hairdriers ('I've got three in case one goes wrong'). She charges £5. 'You have to find a middle of the road price,' she says. 'I haven't put up my price for two years but I notice people thinking twice about paying £5 for a haircut. At the moment I'm not very busy and I know that my hairdresser isn't very busy. It's all to do with the climate of the times, money is tight. It just depends how people look at it, how they value it.' Hairdressers' charges are very different around the country: in London £5 for a haircut is quite reasonable. It gives Sharon M a good living even though she never knows from week to week, even from day to day, how busy she will be. She might not work at all, she might cut six lots of hair. It can be very demanding. Good training is obviously invaluable because 'it gives you the confidence to see through what you're going to do with the hair. If you've got good training that carries you through because you get all sorts of reactions from people. I've had people walk out crying and the next day ring me up and say, "I'm sorry, it's marvellous," and that kind of thing is quite upsetting. This is where confidence in the work and the standard really carries me through.'

Eight months later
'I've kept some of my old clients,' says Sharon M, 'but I'm doing more home visits now. I've also started cutting hair in the evening, some people seem to prefer that . . . It makes a great difference having the extra room in the flat, I can go in there and shut the door. It's far less disturbing.'

Part-time
Capital: none
hairdriers cost between £10 and £20
the 'salon' in her flat cost £100 for the floor and £20 for the sink
Income: A
Qualifications: six-month course at Vidal Sassoon

NURSING

Most freelance nursing is hospital nursing. The agencies filter and sift would-be freelance nurses through to the hospitals. That is the way one system works. In recent years the hospitals have started an alternative system of nurse banks: a pool of nurses attached to one hospital who can be called on at any time to relieve or supplement the regular staff. A few nurses work privately but most are employed, one way or another, by the N.H.S.

Since qualifying as an S.R.N. Paula S has worked for a nursing agency. She has done, or is about to do, all sorts of things: travel, study sociology and economics and, at the moment, work on the administrative side of her agency, the non-profit making London and Provincial Nursing Service. She may well return to nursing in the end, a lot of nurses do. But, in the meantime, after three years of training and six months as a staff nurse with her training hospital Paula S has no intention of committing herself to a full-time job. 'I love nursing,' she says, 'I really do. But I felt I should do something else. I felt dim, dull and dowdy. I didn't know of any particular hospital where I wanted to go and work for any length of time and I didn't want to have an interview, look round and say, "O.K. I'll come and work here." I just couldn't face it.' That was how she felt. Other nurses may have different reasons. 'We have quite a number of mums who want to keep their hand in,' says Paula S, 'do a little bit of work, a couple of nights, a couple of odd days. They've perhaps worked for several years in the National Health beforehand. We've got others who come over from Australia and New Zealand who want to do several months. Sometimes they like it here and they stay. We have nurses who want to come in and have a holiday post or nurses studying for an exam.' Whatever the reason many freelance nurses eventually go back to full-time posts in the N.H.S.

Hospitals, of course, are mostly staffed by full-time nurses but there will probably always be a need for part-time and freelance nurses, especially in the larger cities. The demand for nurses is never completely steady from week to week, month to month, as regular nurses go on holiday, go sick, leave or need reinforcing at weekends and other times. Hospitals have not always seen it this way. 'At one time,' says Paula S, 'hospitals would do all they could not to take on agency nurses but, in that respect, the situation has improved for the freelance. Another thing is that agency nurses have to receive the same statutory pay as other nurses in the N.H.S. This April nurses received a £6 a week pay rise so agency nurses received £6 a week extra.'

From the hospitals' point of view agency nurses have

always been more expensive and less committed than other nurses, which is a major reason for the introduction of nurse banks. There is a chronic shortage of money in the N.H.S. and, until this is resolved, hospitals will be trimming their nursing quotas to the minimum. This affects all nurses, not only freelance ones. Once in a hospital nurses get worked off their feet. 'Understaffing is really a problem,' says Paula S. 'When I was a staff nurse we had just about enough staff, but other parts of the hospital were always borrowing our nurses. Back trouble is an occupational hazard. But because the economic situation is cold people are not leaving their jobs. Everybody is sitting tight and choice is poor everywhere. Wards are being closed in hospitals for lack of money. Things in the future aren't going to be so easy.'

Six months later
Paula S has left London and Provincial Nursing Service, has travelled abroad for three months and is about to start a sociology and economics course. She also fitted in a two-week nursing stint. 'I found work very easily,' she says, 'because I was prepared to work during the day; most people want to work at night. I got the impression there wasn't that much work available, but they were very glad to find dependable people to take it.'

Part-time
Capital: none
Income: £1.45 an hour (days), £1.75 (nights) – S.R.N. rates
Qualifications: S.R.N. or other recognized nursing qualifications

TOURIST GUIDE

Tourism, a lively industry, is well and truly here to stay. Many tourists manage to get around on their own perfectly well; others prefer to sightsee surrounded by their compatriots and escorted by a guide who, besides shepherding them in and out of their coaches, will be a walking encyclopaedia, plumb full of English history and information on museums, pubs, transport, theatres and shopping. Paul S is one such guide. During the season from April to September he is on call as a London guide, ferrying tourists around London and anywhere within a day's drive: Stratford, Oxford, Cambridge, Canterbury, Windsor. His services officially cost £15 a day, that is the rate laid down by the Guild of Guide Lecturers which is campaigning for the full rate for qualified guides and the withdrawal of undercutting unqualified guides. It is a controversial subject. The London Tourist Board, for example, runs a six-month qualifying course but travel agencies and others also employ unqualified guides for less pay. There are other courses around the country and an aspiring guide should go on one if possible. Paul S says so and he has been a qualified guide for two years.

For six months of the year Paul S, if he is lucky, will be worked off his feet; for the rest of the year he will be virtually unemployed except for the antiques business which supplements his income. Work comes through the Guild (which acts as his agent), the L.T.B. or personal recommendation. It is a job which demands the endurance and patience of an elephant and the capacity to satisfy never-ending curious questions. 'A guide,' says Paul S, 'has to be calm, has to be kind. It could be summed up in "be kind".' It also helps to be fluent in a modern language or two and to have the instincts of a teacher, 'to enjoy absorbing knowledge and giving it out again,' he says. 'It's rather like teaching in that way.'

Besides tourists, Paul S also takes round groups of businessmen here on conferences, 'with a couple of days free for visits. Or I pick them up from the airport, take them around for a day or two and drive them back to the airport.' Business trips can mean extra research for the guide, as when 'a group of Americans were coming over in June to look at the docks – the whole area up for redevelopment – and I wrote off to the Ministry asking for information. There are things like this which you have to do for yourself.' Most of his work is with tourists, usually American or European. 'There are three types of American tourist,' Paul S says. 'There is the rich man coming to this country who really wants to get to know it. He probably buys a house and stays some time. The next kind comes over for two to three weeks. The first stop will probably be Shannon, round the ring of Kerry, to Dublin, Glasgow or Edinburgh, followed by the Lakes or York, North Wales, Heart of England, Bath and London. The third type is on a grand tour of Europe and comes to London for three or four days. He'll go on day trips and be booked into the Palladium, a theatre or a night club.' And the European tourist? 'Much more discerning. Germans are particularly good tourists, they want to know what makes this place tick. The French don't always like each other, never mind liking us. The Italians find it difficult to get money out of their country but they manage to come somehow. Of course now the pound is falling England is a very attractive place for Europeans and they come to buy.'

Part-time (six months of year)
Capital: none
Income: B
Qualifications: London Tourist Board examination (see local tourist boards for information)
one or two European languages

MINI-CABS

David B had a brilliant career as an opera singer; he was in full flood when, at the age of twenty-four, he woke up to find his voice had disappeared. 'The voice was in shreds,' he says. 'It was a dreadful time, a singer without a voice is a desolate creature.' With a family to support, 'I thought, well, pull out some of your other resources.' He sold vacuum cleaners. He went into acting. 'I did everything but sing for six or seven years. I did rep for a year, I did old-time music hall, I was the third man in a knockabout busking act. I worked in West End musicals, I did television, never sang a note.' He also ran a decorating business and sold insurance. 'To work for yourself you've got to want to do it very much,' he says, 'because, although you get all the credits, all the benefits, there's nowhere the buck can go, the buck stops here, whether it's financially, artistically, no matter what.'

The voice came back, opera work came back, but nevertheless 'it was a blessing when my voice disappeared because it gave me enormous strength and resourcefulness,' he says. 'Once upon a time I would have sat down and cried. But you become resilient, you can work your way round things.' Nowadays David B only accepts the roles he wants to sing. 'I would rather be independent of theatre work so I have this little business.'

This little business is the mini-cab firm which he and his three partners started six months ago. All the partners have previously worked as mini-cab drivers. 'I initially started driving as a mini-cab driver so I could get off for rehearsals,' he says. 'One has to have a four-door car which is reasonably new. But I was getting into a rut because I had to conform to the hours which the guv'nor wanted me to.' When he and his partners found an office they left to start up on their own. David B is the only one with another occupation – singing – and that comes first; the business fits round it, but it is in no way just a standby job. 'In many ways I'm very business conscious,' he says. 'I like doing the things which use me up. I still work quite hard but I work the hours that suit me.' The partners all cover different aspects. 'I'm the trouble-shooter,' David B says, 'I sort out the problems, do the finances, administration, try and get contracts. Someone else engages the drivers, another one sorts out the cars if they get problems. Another person is there basically to do long hours.' They all do some driving, picking up people and parcels. 'We are the alternative service, quite a different function from the black cab. We'll go anywhere, go long distances, book in advance, doesn't matter. We also do light removals by van.' There are a few regulations governing the use of mini-cabs: one of these is a requirement to keep the car looking like any other, i.e., no lights, phone numbers or notices. The abuse of this law by mini-cab firms gets the regular taxi service up in arms. 'Of course the black cabs are justified in grousing,' says David B. 'They spend a year or two learning routes; it's hard graft and it's expensive. They're entitled to the privileges that they have. There is a place for both.'

Back in the office the controller sits by the telephone taking orders during the day and night. Each driver supplies his own car, insured for 'Hire and Reward' (£80 upwards) and pays the office a commission on his fare of 25p a mile. The business thus acts like an agency. Each partner keeps his own driving money and the drivers' commission initially pays the office expenses including the wages of the controller. The G.P.O., predictably slow, will not be giving them a radio line for another six months.

David B finds clients. 'I do a soft, careful sell,' he says. 'There's not much passing trade so we have regular clients. We do deliveries for factories; we also do all the work for some public houses and individuals. The first call a person makes is the time to consolidate the business; they must become one of your customers.' The way to retain a customer is good service: good driving, time-keeping, presentable car and driver, not overcharging. David B insists his drivers open the car door. 'The critical thing', he says, 'is "Will they be looked after?" If you can supply that, you'll have them coming back again and again. For example, yesterday evening there was a collection of teenage girls who go to dances and who all come back to the same area. They won't get a driver who is either going to overcharge them or play about with them. They know they're going to be all right.'

Eight months later
The mini-cab business is improving all the time and getting a name for itself in North London. As a result the two partners (reduced from four) are getting less pub work and more better paid work, such as contracts for driving to and from the airport. They have recently bought the lease of their premises and have settled in.

Full-time at the moment
Capital: £150 from each partner at the beginning
£750 a year rent for premises
£22 a week for part-time controllers
£70 a week covers overheads such as rent, wages of controllers, phone, electricity. (The drivers' commission is about £60 a week)
four-door saloon car; one driver has van
Income: C
Qualifications: driving licence

ASTROLOGY

Astrology is the study of celestial bodies, planets and stars and their effect on life on this earth, especially individual human life. An astrologer's job is to construct and interpret horoscopes. It's a job which has been on the go for thousands of years and today's astrologers, like Martin F, continue a long tradition. Like many Geminis, so it is said, he enjoys more than one occupation at any time; as advertising manager for a large brewery Martin F controls millions of pounds and as freelance astrologer he works in the evenings on individual horoscopes or on a book he is writing about the sun-sign Aquarius. An aunt originally interested him in astrology. 'She fed me information on anything weird you can think of,' he says; 'she even fed me books on flying saucers when I was in the airforce. When my daughter was born she said, "Oh, let me give her a birthday present of a horoscope," and that was fascinating. I had my chart done.'

Later on, Martin F went to astrology classes and took the Faculty of Astrological Studies correspondence course. Armed with a diploma in 1972, he was able to construct charts professionally. But there is a world of difference between knowing the basic information and being able to apply it, between the newspaper horoscopes, superficial and misleading as they are, and a recognition of astrology as a universal guide. 'Astrology can be used at many levels,' says Martin F, 'but I believe its most important use is as an aid to self-understanding and the need for people to understand the way they fit into the overall pattern. One likes to be able to point people in a direction which will help them grow, increase their awareness, their consciousness and assist in their search at whatever level that search is. The chart can be a very meaningful starting-off point.'

Martin F is personally interested in the movement of the planet from Pisces to Aquarius, in reincarnation and in Jungian analysis, which he is undergoing. Not all astrologers share the same beliefs. Some are quite happy to answer questions like, 'When should I take my holidays?' Others specialize in predicting movements on the stock market, writing books or giving lectures and, of course, there is a gulf of expertise and experience between a £2 horoscope advertised in a magazine such as *Prediction* and a beautifully presented £40 chart. Martin F keeps his work simple and charges £8; he draws up a natal chart based on date, time and place of birth. 'They give me these details,' he says, 'and I try and find out why they want the chart done. They may say, "I'm having awful relationship problems," or "I don't know what to do about my career"; that's fine, one knows what to look for. Most people come to an astrologer at a point when, astrologically speaking, there's a lot happening: turbulence, change, depression, etc.'

Then, a few days later, astrologer and client meet for a couple of hours in the evening. They discuss the chart and all its implications. Martin F does not give a written analysis.

'It is nice to have a written thing that you can refer to from time to time,' he says, 'but my typing is bad and slow and most people seem quite happy to bring along a tape recorder or they take notes.' These sessions are essential for him, he says, because 'this is where you learn and develop as an astrologer, by having people sitting down with you, telling you their problems and you trying to help them.' It is not work to undertake lightly, bordering as it does on medicine and therapy, and it is probably not full-time work either, except for a few well-established astrologers. At any rate Martin F is staying with his job for the time being.

Eight months later
'I finished the book on time and it's being published in Italy, but goodness knows how the money is going to get out of the country, there's such financial chaos. I've recently cut down my work with the Astrological Association, though I still teach one evening a week at the Faculty of Astrological Studies. I'm also taking two evenings for group therapy which I think will help with the consultations.'

Part-time
Capital: none
no separate premises
Income: A
Qualifications: from Faculty of Astrological Studies

Bibliography

GENERAL

Newspaper Press Directory (Benn Bros Ltd, London, 1976).

Trade Associations and Professional Bodies of the United Kingdom, ed. P. Millard (Pergamon, Oxford, 1971).

Directory of British Associations (C.B.D. Research Ltd, Beckenham, Kent).

Current British Directories (C.B.D. Research Ltd).

Handbook of Colleges and Departments of Education (Lund Humphries, London, 1976).

The Bolton Report, Report of the Committee of Inquiry on Small Firms, Command Paper 4811 (H.M.S.O.).

YOUR OWN BUSINESS

Small Businesses, Philip Clarke (David & Charles, Newton Abbot, 1972).

How to be Your Own Boss, Hugh Kinnaird (Hutchinson, London, 1975).

Run Your Own Business, Peter Douglas (J.M. Dent, London, 1973).

Working for Yourself, G. Golzen (Kogan Page, London, 1975).

Guide to Self Employment and Retirement Occupations (Cornmarket Press, London, 1970).

Going Solo (B.B.C. Publications, London, 1975).

See articles in the Business News section of the *Sunday Times*; also the *Financial Times*, the *Daily Telegraph*, *Management Today* and occasionally in *The Guardian*.

CAREERS AND JOBS

Daily Telegraph Careers A–Z (Collins, London, 1975).
Directory of Opportunities for Graduates (Haymarket, London, 1975).
Careers for Girls, Ruth Miller (Penguin, Harmondsworth, 1975).
The Directory of Summer Jobs in Britain, ed. S. Hunt (Vacation Work, 9 Park End Street, Oxford, 1975).
The Directory of Summer Jobs Abroad, ed. C. Moor (Vacation Work, 1976).
Jobs and Careers Abroad, R. Brown (Vacation Work, 1975).

PLANTS AND ANIMALS

Grower Annual and Buyer's Guide (Grower Publications Ltd, 49 Doughty Street, London, WC1), £6. Essential reference for horticulturists: wholesalers, trade associations, marketing, etc.
Practical Self Sufficiency, bimonthly, 50p (Widdington, Saffron Walden, Essex).
The Vegetarian, monthly, 10p (53 Marloes Road, London, W8 Tel. 01–937 7739). Small ads for market gardens, restaurants, etc.

PAPER AND PICTURES

The Professional Practice of Design, Dorothy Goslett (Batsford, London, 1971). For freelance designers.
Picture Researcher's Handbook, Evans and Nelki (David & Charles, Newton Abbot, 1975).
Research: a handbook for writers and journalists, A. Hoffman (Midas Books, 1975).
The Other Careers, Bygrave, Goodman and Fordham (Wildwood House, London, 1973). See chapter on photography.

Writers and Artists Yearbook (A. & C. Black, London).

SHOPS AND SELLING

British Antiques Yearbook, ed. M. d'argy Smith (Michael Joseph, London, 1976).
Markets Year Book (World's Fair Ltd, Union Street, Oldham). Details, rules, regulations, wholesalers.
Export Made Easy (CoSIRA, 35 Camp Road, London SW19 Tel. 01–946 5101), 50p.
Export Handbook (British Overseas Trade Board, 1 Victoria Street, London SW1 Tel. 01–222 7877).

HOUSE AND HOME

Reader's Digest Complete Do-it-Yourself Manual (Reader's Digest Association, 1974). Book 1: techniques; Book 2: projects.
Do-it-Yourself, monthly, 20p (Copyright Link House Publications Ltd, Link House, Dingwall, Croydon, Surrey).
Practical Householder, monthly, 20p (I.P.C. Magazines Ltd, Fleetway House, Farringdon Street, London EC4).
Garnstone Press have a mending and restoring series; see also similar series by Macdonald and Evans.
Mend Your Own China and Glass, Susan Wells (G. Bell & Sons Ltd, London, 1975).

CHILDREN AND TEACHING

How to Form a Playgroup, ed. E. Molony (B.B.C. Publications, London, 1970).

CRAFTS, EATING AND ENTERTAINING

The Craft Business, Rosemary Pettit (Pitman Publishing, London, 1975). Directory for craftsmen: societies, courses, tools, publications, business methods, grants, workshops. See chapter on puppets.
Crafts and Craftsmen, Bruce Alexander (Croom Helm, London, 1974).

SERVICES

Write to the organizations listed in the Names and Addresses section for their leaflets.

Names & Addresses

GENERAL

Smaller Businesses Association, Europe House, World Trade Centre, London E1 Tel. 01–481 8669. Conferences, seminars, advice on industrial relations, export/import, sources of finance. Monthly newsletter. Membership £20.

The Institute of Small Business, Tower Suite, 1 Whitehall Place, London SW1 Tel. 01–930 4001. Ideas and advice on business opportunities; members subscribe either to *Business Ideas Letter* (£13.50) or *Bricks and Mortar* (£12).

National Federation of Self-Employed, 32 St Annes Road West, St-Annes-on-Sea, Lancashire Tel. St Annes 727075. Membership £12.

Small Firms Information Centre, 65 Buckingham Palace Road, London SW1 Tel. 01–828 2384. Nine regional centres. Free government service. Publishes useful booklets: *Starting a Retail Business, Raising Finance for New Enterprises, Obtaining a Franchise, Marketing, Starting in Business, Finding Commercial Information* and several others.

Department of Trade and Industry, 1 Victoria Street, London SW1 Tel. 01–222 7877 and Abell House, John Islip Street, London SW1 Tel. 01–834 4422.

British Institute of Management, Management House, Parker

Street, London WC2 Tel. 01–405 3456. Publications include short 'guide lines' for small business.

The Small Business Centre, Aston Technical, Management and Planning Services Ltd, Alexander Parkes Building, 200 Aston Brook Street, Birmingham Tel. Birmingham 359 4647. Consultancy, research, publications, courses especially for firms in Midlands region.

Council for Small Industries in Rural Areas, 35 Camp Road, London SW19 Tel. 01–946 5101. Technical, managerial and financial help to small firms in rural areas. Similar organizations in Scotland and Northern Ireland.

The Franchise Advisory Centre, 32 Stockwell Park Crescent, London SW9 Tel. 01–737 3553.

Industrial and Commercial Finance Corporation, 91 Waterloo Road, London SE1 Tel. 01–929 7822. Loans from £5,000 to £1 million.

Small Business Capital Fund Ltd, 88 Baker Street, London W1 Tel. 01–486 5021. Loans from £75,000 to £250,000.

Advisory Centre for Education, 32 Trumpington Street, Cambridge Tel. Cambridge 51456. Information service. Publishes *Where*, monthly, £5.50.

National Institute of Adult Education, 35 Queen Anne Street, London W1 Tel. 01–637 4241. Publishes *Year Book of Adult Education* and *Residential Short Courses*.

Association of British Correspondence Colleges, 4 Chiswell Street, London EC1 Tel. 01–606 0255. Represents over twenty colleges.

Training Opportunities Scheme (TOPS) offers 'free training for men and women who want to develop their skills in order to improve their job prospects'. Sixty courses available. Self-employed people are eligible provided they are not in business at the time. Contact local employment office or jobcentre.

PLANTS AND ANIMALS

Farming

Ministry of Agriculture, Fisheries and Food (Publications), Tolcarne Drive, Pinner, Middlesex. Publishes books, maps and leaflets on any crop imaginable. *At the Farmer's Service* is an invaluable reference booklet on government services such as grants; from H.M.S.O.

Agricultural Development and Advisory Service, Great Westminster House, Horseferry Road, London SW1 Tel. 01–216 6681. An advisory service with around thirty regional offices giving free technical and scientific advice to any grower in the area.

Agricultural Training Board, Bourne House, 32-4 Beckenham Road, Beckenham, Kent Tel. 01–650 4890. Leaflets on careers.

National Farmers' Union, Agriculture House, Knightsbridge, London SW1 Tel. 01–235 7853. To promote interests of farmers.

Horticulture

Royal Horticultural Society, Horticultural Hall, Vincent Square, London SW1 Tel. 01–834 4333.

Land Resettlement Association, 43 Cromwell Road, London SW7 Tel. 01–589 9066. Five hundred horticultural small-holdings run as co-operatives; experienced applicants only for tenancies.

Vineyards

English Vineyards' Association Ltd, The Vineyards, Cricks Green, Felsted, Essex. To promote cultivation of vines in U.K.

Organic Farming

Soil Association, Walnut Tree Manor, Haughley, Stowmarket, Suffolk Tel. Haughley 235. Organic farming and gardening. Quarterly review, books, pamphlets, courses.

Henry Doubleday Research Association, 20 Convent Lane, Bocking, Braintree, Essex Tel. Braintree 1483. Organic association. Books and publications; seeds, compost bins, organic pesticides.

Organic Farmers and Growers Ltd, Longridge, Creeting Road, Stowmarket, Suffolk Tel. Stowmarket 2845. Farmers' co-operative for marketing produce of farmers using biological methods.

Working Weekends on Organic Farms, 143 Sabine Road, London SW11 Tel. 01–228 7571. In exchange for working weekends farmers supply food and accommodation to individuals.

Cowley Wood Conservation Centre, Parracombe, Devon Tel. Parracombe 200. Half a dozen short courses a year with practical and theoretical work in organic farming.

Gardening

National Society of Leisure Gardeners, 22 High Street, Flitwick, Bedfordshire. For allotment holders and other gardeners.

London Association of Recreational Gardeners, 34 Ennerdale Avenue, Stanmore, Middlesex. For London gardeners.

Bee-keeping

The British Bee-keepers' Association, 55 Chipstead Lane, River head, Sevenoaks, Kent Tel. Sevenoaks 54873. Many local associations.

Bee Farmers' Association, Mymms House, Gringley-on-the-Hill, Doncaster, Yorkshire Tel. Wiseton 672. For professional bee-keepers.

Breeding

Institute of Fisheries Management, 36 Springfield Road, Wallington, Surrey Tel. 01–647 3967. Eight branches. Meetings, quarterly journal; correspondence course, £25.

Fur Breeders' Association, Beaver Hall, Garlick Hill, London EC4 Tel. 01–248 9095. Looks after interests of mink breeders.

British Chinchilla Breeders' Association, Highfield House, 24 Curzon Park North, Chester.

British Rabbit Council, 302 Farnborough Road, Farnborough, Hampshire.

The Feline Advisory Bureau, Boarding Cattery Information Service, 1 Church Close, Orcheston, Salisbury, Wiltshire. Quarterly bulletin. Welfare, disease and management of cats.

Horses

The British Horse Society, National Equestrian Centre, Stoneleigh, Kenilworth, Warwickshire Tel. Coventry 27192. Advice on training for a career with horses; administers examinations and tests.

Ponies of Britain, Brookside Farm, Ascot, Berkshire Tel. Winkfield Row 2508. To promote the well-being of ponies. Information sheets on, for example, riding stables and trekking centres. Examinations.

PAPER AND PICTURES

Designing

Society of Industrial Artists and Designers, 12 Carlton House Terrace, London SW1 Tel. 01–930 1911. To promote high standards of design for the benefit of the public, industry and commerce. *Designer*, monthly.

The Design Council, 28 Haymarket, London SW1 Tel. 01–839 8000. Displays, exhibitions, competitions. *Design*, monthly. Also Design Council in Cardiff and Glasgow.

Translating

Institute of Linguists, 91 Newington Causeway, London SE1 Tel. 01–407 4755. Professional organization for technical and commercial linguists. Conferences, insurance, information service.

The Translators' Association, 84 Drayton Gardens, London SW10 Tel. 01–373 6642. Literary translating. Members must have at least one work published in U.K.

Indexing

The Society of Indexers, 28 Johns Avenue, London NW4 Tel. 01–203 0929. Safeguards and promotes indexing standards and the professional interests of indexers.

Information Work

Institute of Information Scientists, 657 High Road, London N17 Tel. 01–808 6399. Promotes and maintains high standards in scientific and technical information work.

Aslib, 3 Belgrave Square, London SW1 Tel. 01–235 5050. Specializes in problems related to information collection, retrieval and dissemination. Publishes directory of information sources.

Computer Programming

The British Computer Society, 29 Portland Place, London W1 Tel. 01–637 0471. Learned and professional society for computing practitioners. Thirty-seven branches.

National Computing Centre Ltd, 11 New Fetter Lane, London EC4 Tel. 01–353 4875. To promote the wider and more effective use of computers outside the U.K.

Freelance Programmers Ltd, The Bury, Church Street, Chesham, Buckinghamshire Tel. Chesham 4999. Provides work for freelance programmers.

Market Research

The Market Research Society, 51 Charles Street, London W1 Tel. 01–499 1913. Professional body; sends out list of organizations which employ interviewers.

Association of Market Survey Organizations Ltd, No. 1 De Walden Court, 85 New Cavendish Street, London W1. Trade association; also lists organizations which employ interviewers.

SHOPS AND SELLING

Shopkeeping

Distributive Industry Training Board, Maclaren House, Talbot Road, Stretford, Manchester Tel. Manchester 872 2494. Publishes *Mind Your Own Business*, 70p, for small shopkeepers. Useful information and addresses in free booklets on *Sales Staff, The Buyer, Wholesaling, Jewellery Trade, Grocery Trade, Bookselling, Furniture Trade, Sports Trade, Hardware, Music Trade* amongst others.

National Federation of Retail Newsagents, 2 Bridewell Place, London EC4 Tel. 01–252 6816.

National Federation of Wholesale Grocers and Provisions Merchants, 18 Fleet Street, London EC4 Tel. 01–353 8894. Information for retailers on grocery suppliers.

Bookselling

The Booksellers' Association, 154 Buckingham Palace Road, London SW1 Tel. 01–730 8214. Professional association. Publications include *Opening a Bookshop*, 25p.

Provincial Booksellers' Fairs Association, 19 Pilton Street, Barnstaple, Devon Tel. Barnstaple 3641. For antiquarian and second-hand booksellers.

Illustrating

The Association of Illustrators, 5 Dryden Street, London WC2 Tel 01–898 2781. Bimonthly magazine. Gallery.

Market Trading

National Market Traders' Federation, 87 Spital Hill, Sheffield.

HOUSE AND HOME

Building

The Building Centre, 26 Store Street, London WC1 Tel. 01–637 1022. Ten regional centres. Information and displays of building products and materials.

National Federation of Builders' and Plumbers' Merchants, 15 Soho Square, London W1 Tel. 01–439 1753. Federation of distributors of building materials.

Design

British Institute of Interior Design, 162 Derby Road, Stapleford, Nottingham Tel. Nottingham 39 7250. For information on courses and training.

CHILDREN AND TEACHING

Primary Education

The British Association for Early Childhood Education, Montgomery Hall, Kennington Oval, London SE11 Tel. 01–582 8744. Concerned with children's education and development from birth to eight or nine years old.

Playgroups

Pre-School Playgroups Association, Alford House, Aveline Street, London SE11 Tel. 01–582 8871. Members' association for parents of young children and others interested in the provision of play and educational experience for children under five years. Runs a course on how to organize a playgroup.

Child minding

Contact the Pre-School Playgroups Association (address above) for advice.

CRAFTS

Crafts Advisory Committee, 12 Waterloo Place, London SW1 Tel. 01–839 8000. To 'promote Britain's artist craftsmen'. Exhibitions, information service, index of craftsmen, grants. *Crafts*, bimonthly, 35p.

Council for Small Industries in Rural Areas, 35 Camp Road, London SW19 Tel. 01–946 5101. For information on saddlery, thatching, wrought ironwork, furniture making.

EATING AND ENTERTAINING

Catering

Hotel, Catering and Institutional Management Association, 191 Trinity Road, London SW17 Tel. 01–672 4251. Professional association. Administers one-year full-time course in Institutional Management.

Hotel and Catering Industry Training Board, P.O. Box 18, Ramsey House, Central Square, Wembley, Middlesex Tel. 01–902 8865.

The Brewers' Society, 42 Portman Square, London W1 Tel. 01–486 4831. For information on running a pub and how to apply; organizes and runs residential training schemes.

The Cordon Bleu Cookery School, 114 Marylebone Lane, London W1 Tel. 01–935 3503.

Tante Marie School of Cookery, Woodham House, Carlton Road, Woking, Surrey Tel. Woking 4050.

John Tovey, Miller Howe, Windermere, Cumbria Tel. Windermere 2536. Five-day cookery courses.

Entertainment

Puppet Centre Trust, Battersea Town Hall Community Arts Centre, Lavender Hill, London SW11 Tel. 01–223 5356. Theatre, workshops, information, library.

SERVICES

Hairdressing

The National Hairdressers' Federation, 11 Goldington Road, Bedford Tel. Bedford 53245. Trade organization for salon owners.

The Incorporated Guild of Hairdressers, Wigmakers and Perfumers, 4 The Broadway, Woodbridge Road, Guildford, Surrey Tel. Guildford 37663. Also represents the hairdressing trade; for information on training.

Nursing

The Nursing and Hospital Careers Information Service, 8 Leake Street, London SE1 Tel. 01–402 5296.

The General Nursing Council for England and Wales, 23 Portland Place, London W1 Tel. 01–580 8334.

London and Provincial Nursing Services, York House, 199 Westminster Bridge Road, London SE1 Tel. 01–261 1540.

Tourist Guide

London Tourist Board, 4 Grosvenor Gardens, London SW1 Tel. 01–730 3400.

British Tourist Authority, 64 St James's Street, London SW1 Tel. 01–629 9191. Twelve regional offices.

Guild of Guide Lecturers, 5 Chiswick Lodge, Chiswick Road, London W4 Tel. 01–995 2008. Association of London guides.

Astrology

Faculty of Astrological Studies, Hook Cottage, Vines Cross, Heathfield, Sussex. Classes in London and correspondence courses.

Occupation: Self-Employed

Mayo School of Astrology, Piper's Wood, Slackhead, Beetham, Milnthorpe, Cumbria. Correspondence courses.

Astrological Association, 20 Ensor Mews, London SW7. Lectures, meetings, conferences.